Kartar Singh Duggal (born 1917), nominated to Parliament (Rajya Sabha) as an eminent Indian writer, has to his credit twenty-two collections of short stories, ten novels, two collections of poetry, seven plays, more than fifty short plays, an autobiography and several works of literary criticism. K.S. Duggal has been honoured with the Padma Bhushan, the Soviet Land Nehru Award and Punjab Sahitya Akademi's Sarva-Saresht Sahityakar Award for the totality of his contribution to Indian literature besides the National Academy of Letters Award for short stories, the Ghalib Award for drama, the Bhasha Parishad Award for fiction and the Bhai Mohan Singh Award for autobiography. In recognition of his contribution to Indian literature, Duggal was conferred the degree of D. Litt. (Honoris Causa) by the Punjabi University in 1994. Having served as Director, All India Radio, Director, National Book Trust, and Adviser (Information) in the Planning Commission of India, he is currently devoted exclusively to literary activity.

Other titles by the author
in UBSPD

The Akal Takht
and Other Seats of Sikh Polity

The Sikh People :
Yesterday and Today

The Sikh Gurus :
Their Lives and Teachings

Orphans of the Storm :
Stories on the Partition of India (Co-editor)

Select Sikh Scriptures − I
Guru Nanak

Select Sikh Scriptures – II
Guru Arjan Dev

Compiled and Transcreated
by
Kartar Singh Duggal

🕮 UBSPD
UBS Publishers' Distributors Ltd.
New Delhi ● Mumbai ● Bangalore ● Chennai
Calcutta ● Patna ● Kanpur ● London

UBS Publishers' Distributors Ltd.

5 Ansari Road, New Delhi-110 002
Phones : 3273601, 3266646 ☆ *Cable* : ALLBOOKS ☆ *Fax* : (91) 11-327-6593
e-mail: ubspd.del@smy.sprintrpg.ems.vsnl.net.in
Apeejay Chambers, 5 Wallace Street, Mumbai-400 001
Phones : 2076971, 2077700 ☆ *Cable* : UBSIPUB ☆ *Fax* : 2070827
10 First Main Road, Gandhi Nagar, Bangalore-560 009
Phones : 2263901, 2263902, 2253903 ☆ *Cable* : ALLBOOKS ☆ *Fax* : 2263904
6, Sivaganga Road, Nungambakkam, Chennai-600 034
Phone : 8276355, 8270189 ☆ *Cable* : UBSIPUB ☆ *Fax* : 8278920
8/1-B, Chowringhee Lane, Calcutta-700 016
Phones : 2441821, 2442910, 2449473 ☆ *Cable* : UBSIPUBS ☆ *Fax* : 2450027
5 A, Rajendra Nagar, Patna-800 016
Phones : 672856, 673973, 656170 ☆ *Cable* : UBSPUB ☆ *Fax* : 656169
80, Noronha Road, Cantonment, Kanpur-208 004
Phones : 369124, 362665, 357488 ☆ *Fax* : 315122

© Kartar Singh Duggal

First Published **1998**

Kartar Singh Duggal asserts the moral right to be identified as the author of this work.

Cover Design : Ilaksha

Designed & Typeset at UBSPD in 12 pt Times Roman
Printed at Replika Press (P) Ltd., Delhi (India)

For
My Children
Shehla and Suhel

Acknowledgement

Shri Lalit Sethi, formerly of *The Statesman,* was kind enough to have a close look at the TS and the work has benefited by his suggestions

—K.S.D.

Contents

Introduction

This grandson of mine
Like a ship will cruise
Across the ocean (of life in his time)

GURU AMAR DAS

Guru Arjan was born at Goindwal in 1563. He was the youngest son of Bhai Jetha (later Guru Ram Das) and Bibi Bhani. It is said that there was unusual rejoicing at his birth. This surprised quite a few since the new-born was only the third son of Guru Amar Das' daughter, whereas his sons, Mohan and Mohri, had also been married and not much notice had ever been taken when they had their children. Guru Amar Das was extremely fond of Baba Arjan who, as a child, was always hovering around him. It is said that once during the Guru's afternoon siesta, young Arjan quietly slipped into his room and woke him up. Nobody ever disturbed the Guru during his afternoon nap since he got up very early in the morning for his meditation and prayers. The attendant was nervous and ran to pick up the child from the Guru's chamber. The Guru forbade him and observed —
Eh mera dohta pani da bohitha hovega — this grandson

of mine, like a ship, will cruise across the ocean (of life in his time).

As predicted, when the time came for Guru Ram Das to retire, Arjan Dev was ordained to take over as the fifth Guru.

However, Prithi Chand, Guru Arjan's eldest brother, did not accept him as his father's successor. On the passing away of Guru Ram Das, according to a custom prevalent among the Khatris of the time, when Mohri invested Guru Arjan with the turban, as a symbol of succession, Prithi Chand objected to it vehemently. As the eldest son of Guru Ram Das, he maintained that it was he who ought to have been offered the ceremonial turban. When Guru Arjan came to know of it, he lost no time in presenting the turban to Prithi Chand. Not only this, he also left Goindwal for the new township, which was under construction, to avoid any further unpleasantness. Yet Prithi Chand was not reconciled. He started intriguing and conspiring against the Guru. Guru Arjan did not take much notice of him; he was busy completing the Holy Tanks of Santokhsar at Amritsar as well as the other jobs left unfinished by Guru Ram Das.

It is said that while the excavation at Santokhsar was in progress, the diggers chanced upon a tiny hut in which they found a Yogi squatting in deep contemplation. He was brought out immediately and given a massage. After a little while, he regained consciousness and was delighted to meet Guru Arjan. He said that ages ago he had pleased his Guru who had blessed him and said, "You will meet Guru Arjan in the Kaliyug and attain deliverance at his hands." He had been in meditation ever since.

Santokhsar was completed in 1588.

Guru Arjan now devoted his attention to the completion of Amritsar, the 'Tank of nectar'. He laid the foundation-stone of the Hari Mandir — later known as the Golden Temple. The Sikhs desired that it should be the tallest building in the town. The Guru, however, thought otherwise. He reminded his followers that there was no virtue like humility. The Temple was, therefore, built on as low an elevation as possible. He also decided to have four doors to the Temple, one in each direction. Anyone could enter it from any side. No one would be discri-minated against. For laying the foundation-stone of the Temple, Guru Arjan invited Mian Mir, a Muslim divine from Lahore. With the resources and dedication of the Sikhs, construction of the Holy Tank and the Temple made rapid progress. The Guru sang in joy:

> *God Himself came to participate*
> *And gave His hand in Godmen's task.*
> *He poured nectar in the blessed Tank*
> *Built in the blessed land.*
> *He poured nectar and completed the job,*
> *A dream has come true.*
> *The whole world is hailing.*
> *All fears are set free.*
> *He is all-powerful with ever-living presence,*
> *The Vedas and the Puranas sing His praises.*
> *Nanak has been blessed by God,*
> *Who has meditated on the Lord.*

SUHI

When the Holy Tank was completed, with his characteristic humility, Guru Arjan gave the entire credit for it to Guru Ram Das:

> *A dip in the tank of Ram Das*
> *All my sins are washed away.*
> *A dip and I am clean all over*
> *I've been blessed by Him to whom I pray.*
>
> SORATH

Prithi Chand continued to pester the Guru. He, therefore, decided to leave Amritsar and go out on an extensive tour and meet his disciples in various parts of the Punjab. He visited Khadur, Goindwal, Sarhali, Bhaini, Khanpur, Taran Taran, Lahore, Dera Baba Nanak and several other places. During his tour, he laid the foundation-stone of Kartarpur, a new township near Jalandhar. He also got a well called Ganga Sagar dug in the town.

A popular story revolves around this well. It is said that one day, a pilgrim called Baisakhi, came to see the Guru while on his way to Hardwar. He used to go on pilgrimage to the holy place every year. The Guru told him that taking a bath with the water of the well that had been recently dug in the town could also clean him if he cared. The water, after all, comes from the same source. Baisakhi would not listen to it. He had been going to Hardwar annually for several years and he did not want to miss the pilgrimage that year. The Guru did not pursue the argument. However, after some months when the pilgrims returned, he regretted that the day he was leaving Hardwar his pilgrim's vessel was washed away in the Ganga so he could not bring the Holy Water for the Guru. At this, it is said, the Guru walked up to the new well and fished out Baisakhi's vessel that had slipped from his hands and got lost in the Ganga. Baisakhi was astonished to see the vessel with his name etched on it. He realised the true meaning of 'pilgrimage'

Guru Arjan returned to Amritsar after several months. Prithi Chand was still bitter and the Guru was at a loss to know how to appease him. As it happened, Guru Arjan had no son. Prithi Chand hoped that his own son Mehrban would have a chance to succeed as the next Guru. But disappointment was in store for him again.

Finding his wife keen to have a child, Guru Arjan asked her to go to Bhai Budha for his blessings. Bhai Budha, an associate of Guru Nanak, was revered by the Sikhs and the Guru alike. It was an unheard of expression of humility on the part of the reigning apostle to send his wife to seek the blessings of a Sikh, but she had to adhere to her husband's advice. Accompanied by her attendants, she went in a procession to meet Bhai Budha, who lived in a wood outside the town. Bhai Budha did not approve of all the fanfare. Far from blessing the Guru's wife, he did not even touch the delicacies she had brought by way of offerings for him. She was utterly disappointed. When the Guru came to know of it, he told her to go again with simple food cooked with her own hands and with the humility of a devotee. The next day she did accordingly.

Bhai Budha was delighted to partake of her simple fare and, while crushing an onion with his fist, said,

"The son that you will have will crush the enemies the way I have crushed the onion. He will be a great sportsman, fond of hunting; he will ride royal horses and carry two swords. He will possess both spiritual and temporal powers."

Prithi Chand, in the meanwhile, cultivated the friendship of Sulhi Khan, a revenue officer of the Mughal court, and instigated him to raid Amritsar on the pretext of collecting tax dues. Since Guru Arjan's wife was expecting a baby, he decided to retire to a village close by, leaving Amritsar to Prithi Chand to settle account with Sulhi Khan.

During his stay at Wadali, Guru Arjan found that due to scarcity of water, the people of the village were put to a great deal of inconvenience. He, therefore, had a huge well dug up with the voluntary help of the Sikhs. It was large enough to accommodate six Persian wheels. The place has since come to be known as Chherata — the town of six Persian wheels.

It was at Wadali that a son was born to Guru Arjan, in 1595. There was great rejoicing in Amritsar at the happy news. To commemorate Bhai Budha's blessings, a fair is held every year in the wood where he used to live. Childless women who go to participate in the congregation held on the occasion of the fair, are believed to be blessed with children. The more the Sikhs rejoiced on the birth of Hargobind — that was the name given to the child — the more unhappy Prithi Chand was. Even his wife Karmo lost her peace of mind. The only hope left to them was to have the new-born killed somehow. Accordingly, they took an old family nurse into confidence, promised her a big reward, and sent her to

Wadali. She had her nipples smeared with poison. Evidently, she was looking for an opportunity to suckle the new-born and poison him to death.

However, the moment she took the child in her lap, she fainted. The poison applied on her nipples seemed to have infected her. The Guru had her immediately attended to and her life was saved. When she came to her senses, she confessed her guilt.

Prithi Chand was undeterred. After some time, he asked a snake-charmer to release a poisonous serpent in Guru Arjan's courtyard where the child normally played. The toddler, it is said, picked up the snake and started playing with it.

The devotees came from distant places to Amritsar to pay their homage to the Guru and, not finding him there, were greatly disappointed. The Sikhs of the town, therefore, went to the Guru in a deputation and persuaded him to return to the Holy City ignoring what Prithi Chand continued to do.

After a while, Hargobind was stricken with a severe attack of small-pox and Prithi Chand's hopes were revived. Prithi Chand was sure that the child would not survive. But Hargobind recovered from the malady, disappointing his uncle once again.

The only hope for Karmo's son to succeed Guru Arjan was the elimination of Hargobind, and Prithi Chand was persistent in his efforts. He now bribed a domestic servant in the Guru's household to poison the milk the child took. Once again Prithi Chand failed. The child refused to drink the milk the servant offered. When the servant insisted, Hargobind took the bowl of milk and threw it away. It is said, a dog who tried to lap it up died instantly. The domestic servant was questioned and he confessed his guilt. Guru Arjan was greatly distressed by his brother's misdeeds.

Hargobind was fairly grown up now and his father sent him over to Bhai Budha so that he could be groomed for the responsibilities he was destined to shoulder.

Before long another serious development engaged Guru Arjan's attention. Reports came that Prithi Chand was composing his own hymns, and was passing them on to the Sikhs visiting Amritsar, as the compositions of Guru Nanak and other Sikh Gurus. If this was allowed to continue, Guru Arjan feared, it would be the undoing of the Sikh faith. He, therefore, decided to take immediate steps to remedy this malpractice.

He sent his trusted Sikhs like Bhai Piara and others all over the country and himself went to Goindwal, Khadur and Kartarpur with a view to collecting the authentic texts of the *Bani* of the four Gurus preceding him. Mohan, Datu and Sri Chand, some of the collaterats, helped him most in this task. He, then, had a special camp set up by the side of Ramsar tank and started compiling what subsequently came to be known as the Holy Granth. Consistent with the tradition of the Sikh faith, Guru Arjan also collected and incorporated some of the spiritual verses of other Indian saints, both Hindus and Muslims, in the compilation. The hymns were arranged under the specific musical measure or *raga* in which they were originally written by Guru after Guru, in chronological order. The compositions of saints outside Sikhism figured after these. It is said that several poets or their admirers approached the Guru to have their verses included in the Holy Granth under compilation. A few among these were Chhajju, Shah Hussain and Pilu. But it seems their writings did not qualify for inclusion in the *Pothi*.

Bhai Gurdas undertook to prepare the master copy of the compilation. He was also invited by the Guru to contribute his own verses for inclusion in the *Pothi*, but his modesty prevented him from doing so. The compilation was completed in 1604. After the monumental work had been completed to his entire satisfaction, Guru Arjan added this hymn by way of epilogue, in utter humility:

> *I know not Your ways,*
> *Worthy of it all You've made me.*
> *Worthless I was, without any merit,*
> *With Your grace You've swayed me.*
> *Mercifully you took benevolent*
> *And I met the True Guru.*
> *Nanak now lives on the Name alone*
> *His mind and body are blessed, true.*

SLOK V

A large number of miracles are associated with Guru Arjan:

A Sikh called Triloka, who was employed in the army at Kabul, once killed a female deer. The deer happened to be pregnant. It pained Triloka to find the two unborn young ones of the deer also die before his eyes. He pledged not to indulge in hunting any more. Not only this, rather than carry a proper sword, Triloka started donning a sword with a wooden blade. This was unheard of in the fighting forces of the day. Someone complained about it to his commandant, who came for a surprise check of Triloka's arms. Triloka remembered the Guru and prayed for his help in his hour of distress. To his delight when he pulled out the blade from the scabbard, it was shining like steel. Those who had complained against him were embarrassed.

Similarly, Katara, another Sikh from Kabul, happened to be in trouble. Someone wanting to do him harm replaced his weights and complained to the authorities that he was using short weights. His premises were raided by the police for inspection. The innocent Sikh invoked the Guru's help in his hour of peril. It is said that at the same moment, Guru Arjan was made an offering of some coins at Amritsar. He held the weight of the coins for a while in his right palm and then in the left palm. He shifted the coins from one palm to the other again and again. When asked by the devotees why he did this, he told them about Katara who was involved in a false case in far-away Kabul and was craving for his help. The next time Katara visited Amritsar he corroborated every word that the Guru had told his Sikhs.

Chandu Shah, a Hindu banker of Delhi, who wielded a lot of influence at the Mughal court, was looking for a suitable hand for his daughter. He was originally from the Punjab and was keen that the groom should be a Punjabi youth. His emissaries went all over the Punjab but did not find an eligible match. Eventually, on their way back, they happened to visit Amritsar and saw Hargobind, the young son of Guru Arjan. Besides being handsome and healthy, he was to succeed his father. The agents hurried back to Delhi to inform Chandu Shah. He, however, had the ego of a spoilt courtier. He could not imagine giving his daughter in marriage to anyone, what he considered, below his status. "At best, he lives on the offerings of his followers," he objected. "He has no social or political status. A brick baked for a palace cannot be used for a gutter." The agents were silenced. The proposal was accordingly dropped. In the meanwhile, the Sikhs of Delhi came to know of Chandu Shah's remarks and they conveyed these duly to the Guru. The agents continued to look around but they could not find a suitable hand for Chandu Shah's daughter. The marriageable daughter became the source of grave anxiety to the mother. She could not wait any longer. She felt that Hargobind was an excellent match for their daughter and that they should not have turned down the proposal. Before long Chandu Shah also realised his mistake and sent for the agents and asked them to finalise the proposal. The agents went to Amritsar. But the Guru, who had been informed about Chandu Shah's earlier remarks, declined to accept the offer. He said that the daughter of a rich man like Chandu Shah would not fit into the house of a *darvesh*. Chandu Shah could not imagine that the hand of his daughter could be refused by anyone. He was wild to see the proposal and gifts returned to him. In a fury of temper he decided to avenge the indignity hurled on him.

Soon an opportunity came his way. Prithi Chand, the Guru's eternal enemy, complained to him that the *Pothi* compiled by the Guru had derogatory references to Muslim and Hindu prophets and saints. Chandu Shah lost no opportunity in bringing this fact to the notice of the Emperor. Akbar issued an order that the Guru and the *Pothi* be immediately produced before him. Guru Arjan sent Bhai Budha and Bhai Gurdas to the Mughal court with a copy of the *Pothi*. When the compilation was opened, the first hymn read out was:

> *From clay and light God created the world.*
> *The sky, the earth, trees and water are conceived*
>   *by Him.*
> *I have seen men pass away.*
> *Forgetting God in avarice is like eating carrion,*
> *The way the evil spirits kill and devour the dead.*
> *One must restrain oneself;*
> *Hell is the punishment otherwise.*
> *The miracle man, the riches, brothers, courtiers,*
>   *kingdom and palaces,*
> *None will come to your rescue at the hour of*
>   *departure,*
> *When the messenger of death comes to carry you.*
> *God, the Pure, knows what's in store for me*
> *Nanak, my appeal of a slave is alone to you.*
>
> TILANG

The Emperor heard it and was fully satisfied. He had always looked upon the Sikh Gurus as social reformers and believers in the unity of God and the brotherhood of man. And all this was close to his heart.

However, Chandu Shah, who had considerable influence in the court, was too wicked to be satisfied. He said that Bhai Gurdas, who had read the hymn, had done so from memory and had not read the text from the *Pothi*. He, therefore, got one Sahib Dyal from the town and made him read for them another piece from a page of his own choice. The hymn read out this time was:

> *You don't see God who dwells in your heart,*
> *And you carry about an idol around your neck.*
> *A non-believer, you wander about churning water,*
> *And you die harassed in delusion.*
> *The idol you call God will drown with you.*
> *The ungrateful sinner!*
> *The boat will not ferry you across.*
> *Says Nanak, I met the Guru who led me to*
> *   God.*
> *He who lives in water, earth, netherregion,*
> *   firmament and across.*

SUHI

The Emperor was delighted to listen to the hymn. It was as nobly inspired as the earlier piece. Far from finding anything that could be construed as maligning anyone, he felt that the hymn inculcated love and devotion and strove to rid both the Hindus and the Muslims of communalism that was tearing them apart. It was exactly this which he wished to project through Din-i-Ilahi, a new religion he advocated.

The Emperor was happy to be acquainted with the highly inspiring volume compiled by the Guru. He bestowed robes of honour on Bhai Budha and Bhai Gurdas and sent one for Guru Arjan along with numerous gifts. He also promised to pay his respects personally to the Guru when he visited Lahore next.

The Emperor kept his promise and came on pilgrimage to Amritsar. He was greatly impressed with the activities of the Guru. He made rich offerings and sought the Guru's blessings for the peace and welfare of his kingdom. At the Guru's intervention, the Emperor exempted the region from land revenue as it had suffered a severe drought that year. When the cultivators came to know of it they were deeply grateful to the Guru.

Unfortunately, a monarch of vision like Akbar did not live long. His son Jehangir occupied the throne though Akbar, at one time, wanted to nominate his grandson Khusro to succeed him.

Jehangir was a libertine, fond of wine and hunting. He left the administration of the kingdom to his Queen and his courtiers. While on his way to Kashmir for a holiday, the Emperor summoned Guru Arjan to meet him in Lahore mainly at Chandu Shah's instigation.

When the Guru received the Emperor's summons he knew what was in store for him. He called Hargobind and had him installed as the sixth Guru in the presence of prominent Sikhs. As per the practice Bhai Budha applied the *tilak* on Hargobind's forehead. The Guru, then, took leave of his Sikh disciples and bidding farewell to his beloved city of Amritsar, left for Lahore.

The Emperor levied a fine of Rupees Two lakhs and asked the Guru to revise the *Pothi* deleting all references to Islam and Hinduism figuring in it. The Guru told Jehangir that his money was the sacred trust of the Sikh community and the hymns in the Holy Granth were a revelation in praise of God; no one dare alter them.

The Emperor was on his way to Kashmir. He was in a hurry and in no mood to involve himself in arguments. He asked Murtaza Khan, the local administrator, to deal with the Guru the way he considered best and proceeded on his journey. It was exactly the opportunity Chandu Shah was looking for. He approached Murtaza Khan and poisoned his ears urging him to extract the fine levied by the Emperor.

The moment the Sikhs of Lahore came to know that the Guru had been put in prison for non-payment of the fine, they started collecting funds. When Guru Arjan heard of it, he forbade them to do so. He had done no wrong for which he should pay a fine. In the meanwhile, the *qazi* gave his injunction ordering the Guru to be tortured to death, in case he didn't agree to expunge the so-called derogatory reference to Islam and Hinduism from the *Pothi*.

It is said that the Guru was made to sit on a red-hot iron sheet. They poured burning hot sand on his body; he was also given a dip in boiling water. As the Guru was being persecuted thus, Mian Mir, the Muslim divine of Lahore who had laid the foundation-stone of the Holy Temple at Amritsar, came and begged the Guru, seeking permission to use his mystic power to punish those who were responsible for inflicting suffering upon him. The Guru heard Mian Mir and counselled patience. He told him that one must accept the will of God; not even a leaf can move if God does not ordain it. When Chandu Shah's daughter-in-law heard about it, she bribed the jailer and came to the prison with *sherbet* and other delicacies to serve the Guru. The Guru declined to accept anything from Chandu Shah's house but blessed the lady for her faith and devotion.

The Guru was tortured for five long days. When the tyrants found him bearing all the agony with perfect equanimity, they became helpless. They were at a loss and did not know what to do. The Guru then sought permission for taking a bath in the river Ravi which flowed by the side of the Mughal fort where he was imprisoned. Thousands of his followers watched the Guru walk to the river with tears in their eyes. His bare body glistened with blisters. There were blisters on his feet and he could not even walk properly. "Sweet is your will, O God, the gift of Your Name alone I ask," recited the Guru again and again. As he reached the river, he bade farewell to the bewailing multitude and walked into the water as serene and as calm as ever. It is said that it was the last glimpse his devotees had of the Guru. He never came out of the river. The tide bore him in her longing lap and he was gone for ever. Guru Arjan was only 43 years old at the time of his supreme sacrifice on 30 May, 1606.

Thus a magnificent life was brutally cut short by the hands of tyranny. The way Guru Arjan sacrificed his life for the values that he cherished is of far-reaching significance. With his martyrdom a transformation came in the thinking of the Sikh community. Emulating their Guru, they would readily give their lives for any cause dear to them — whether it was a fight with the bigoted rulers of the day for the protection of their faith, or with the British for the freedom of their country.

Guru Arjan's humility is almost unparalleled. There was no trace of ego; he maintained that more important than the Guru are the Guru's Sikhs. What they decide in a congregation must hold good. Since the Delhi Sikhs did not want the Guru's son to be married to Chandu Shah's daughter because of Chandu Shah's arrogance, the Guru respected their wishes even when his life was at stake.

The Sikh, Gurus established places of worship called *dharamsalas* and promoted projects of general welfare like digging of wells, *baolies* and tanks. They set up new villages and townships. With a view to fighting social evils, they encouraged common kitchens and community living. They were poets and music lovers. They patronised arts and artists. While Bhai Mardana, the rabab player, was a constant companion of Guru Nanak, Satta and Balwand and a number of other professional musicians were attached to the Gurus who followed Nanak. They would have indeed been happy if they were left alone to pursue their mission of propagating the veneration of God and the love of man to the people of the world.

To a student of Guru Arjan's life, the Guru's martyrdom was a certainty. The forces of evil and hatred were relentless and the events' moved with calamitous inevitability. The Guru had attended to all his major assignments. The completion of the Holy Tank called Amritsar, and the Hari Mandir, known as the Golden Temple, gave the Sikh community a sense of solidarity. The town which came up around the Holy Tank grew into a metropolis of the Sikhs all over the world. The *Pothi* not only preserved the Holy Word; it has served as a spiritual lighthouse ever since its compilation. In his not too long life of 43 years, Guru Arjan's achievements were monumental. He could accomplish all this maybe because he was groomed for his mission by his maternal grandfather and then by his own father. His predecessors Guru Angad, Guru Amar Das and Guru Ram Das did not have this advantage.

Though a man of letters and a poet of eminence, Guru Arjan was highly organised and practical. Since he undertook massive construction works, he set up brick kilns to bake bricks. With a view to making Amritsar a self-sufficient town, he invited skilled workers of all crafts to settle there along with traders from Kashmir and Kabul. He thus, succeeded in making Amritsar an important commercial centre in the Punjab.

A soldier once came to the Guru for spiritual advice. Guru Arjan told him that as long as he served in the army, he must remain loyal to the king and fight his enemies. A soldier's dharma is to live for peace and die fighting.

Guru Nanak had rejected the caste system of the Hindus. "There is no higher caste," he said, "and there is no lower caste. It is one's deeds that determine whether one is good or bad, high or low." Guru Arjan sought to abolish the distinction between the haves and the have-nots (the caste-system that permeated the economic sphere), those who laboured and those who exploited them. He did not attach any great importance to contemplative life if it had to be sustained on the sweat of the neighbour's brow. He advised that one must work and earn and share one's earning with others.

The Hindu theory of *Karma* upholds that what we are is of our own making. We suffer because of misdeeds committed in our previous life. So even the indignities and atrocities inflicted by the rulers were borne by the Hindus with stoic indifference; Guru Arjan said that evil must be resisted, even if one has to lay down one's life for it. He underlined the virtues of self-sacrifice even if it means giving away one's life.

Guru Arjan was highly practical in day-to-day conduct. Once a village headman called Chuhar came to him for his blessings. He believed that the nature of his duties was such that he had to resort to falsehood. He was anxious to know how he was going to find his deliverance. The Guru asked him to maintain a record of his good and bad deeds and bring it over to him at the end of the month. When Chuhar came after a month, it was discovered that he had hardly done any good deed, whereas he had a large number of bad deeds to his credit. The Guru asked him to read them out and confess his sins in public. The next month his performance was better. It improved consistently in the following months, until the village headman had all the good deeds to his credit and not one bad deed.

Accepting the Will of God, Guru Arjan gave up his life suffering inhuman atrocities. Yet the last message he sent to his son was to arm himself fully and prepare for the struggle ahead which was to be a long drawn-out war against tyranny.

In Guru Arjan we have the acme of Guru Nanak's message. After his revelation at Sultanpur on the banks of the river Bain, Guru Nanak's utterance — There is no Hindu; there is no Musalman — was aimed at ushering in a new way of life in the conflict-torn land of Hindus where the Muslim conquerors had come to make their home. Since he could not fulfil his mission in his life-span, Guru Nanak had to reincarnate himself in his successors one after the other.

Guru Arjan was the fifth in succession. As the compiler of the Holy Granth, he conceptualised the Sikh creed and classified and recorded the Sikh Scriptures. Unlike his predecessors who had to be elevated, being the son of a Guru himself, he was groomed and perfectly equipped for the exalted task. His contribution to the Holy Granth is the largest: 2218 hymns as against 974 of Guru Nanak, 62 of Guru Angad, 907 of Guru Amar Das, 679 of Guru Ram Das and 166 of Guru Tegh Bahadur. Guru Arjan's ministry acquires added significance because it marks the end of an era in Sikh perceptions. Considering the political climate of the times, his successor, Guru Hargobind combined *Piri* (piety) with *Miri* (polity); the saints of Guru Nanak turned into saint-soldiers, a concept which found its ultimate expression in Guru Gobind Singh's relentless fight against the unjust and high-handed rule of the day.

A poet of rare excellence, Guru Arjan's hymns combine in them vision of a sage and the sensitivity of an artist. *Parbrahma* or the Supreme Being is believed to be *Nirguna* (Transcendent) by some and *Saguna* (Immanent) by others. The former maintain that the Divine Entity is beyond any form while the latter worship the Creator in one or the other form. Guru Arjan provides a synthesis of the two concepts. He believes that all forms are informed by the Formless. The Ultimate Being is inherent in all beings and yet remains transcendent. Guru Arjan does not support the view that the concept of beauty is different from the physical beauty; whereas the physical beauty fades and withers, the beauty in abstract remains ever the same. According to Guru Arjan the physical and the meta-physical, the individual and the Ultimate are essentially integrated. Guru Nanak glorifies the one whom he finds reflected in Nature (*Qudrat Wassiya*) all around. *Nirguna,* he says, is Unattributed while *Saguna* is Attributed. Guru Arjan subscribes to uncompromising monotheism, yet he attributes moral and ethical qualities to the Divine Entity so that the devotee can concretise, appreciate and approach the Lord with loving devotion which has come to be known as *Bhakti.*

The Creator is distinct from the creation and yet the created is a part of the Creator. It is like the wave born out of the ocean destined to merge into it . This is how Guru Arjan visualises the Nirguna (Unattributed) entity of the Divine:

> *He is Absolute and related*
> *The Formless sits in a void in an ecstatic state.*
> *When the creation was not even conceived,*
> *Who was the bad and who was good?*
> *When He was in a meditating trance,*
> *For strife and hatred who had the chance?*
> *When He had no features, no form,*
> *Joy and sorrow then came wherefrom?*
> *When the Supreme Lord was all by Himself,*
> *Who loved whom and who was doubtful?*
> *His is the game and Himself He plays,*

There is no other Creator, thus Guru Nanak says.

SUKHMANI

Guru Arjan refers to Saguna (Attributed) Entity of the Divine thus:

He is fire in the wood and ghee in the milk.
His light prevails in the high and the low.
The Master dwells in every heart.

RAGA SORATH V

And if He so desires, He may undo it all:
When He winds up the show, says Nanak,
He is left all alone.

RAGA MARU

Despite his close relationship with the concept of the Supreme Being, Guru Arjan does not seem to subscribe to the concept of Non-Duality of Shankaracharya as such. The self, according to him, is of Divine essence yet it is not the Infinite. There is a subtle difference. The Sikh monotheistic mysticism is distinct from monism. There are ever so many references to it in Guru Arjan's 'Sukhmani':

He is Nirguna (Unattributed) and also Saguna
  (Attributed)
With His charm He has snared us all.
The Formless is both Nirguna and Saguna,
Himself He is the absolute void.

Himself He brings glory to Himself (in man).
Says Nanak, God and His devotee belong to the
*   same clan.*

And then in 'Raga Bilawal' Guru Arjan is more specific:

I am nothing, everything is Yours, my Lord!
You are Nirguna here and Saguna there
In between my Master plays.

In 'Raga Suhi' Guru Arjan refers to the other aspect:

The way a juggler plays tricks,
Appearing in various figures and features,
He takes off His disguise,
Calls halt to creation
And is left alone, the Lone Creator.

Be that as it may, idol-worship is vehemently decried by Guru Arjan. His grandson, the tenth Sikh Guru, Guru Gobind Singh went to the extent of declaring: "Those who call me the Supreme Being must go to hell". Guru Arjan has faith in the Creator alone:

Ignoring the gracious who worship others,
They are a homicidal lot.
Forgetting the Master they suffer in agony;
They are born and die time and again,
Those who stick not to the Lord.

MALHAR V

Guru Arjan would not have you propitiate anyone other than the Supreme Being. There is, however, an exception. It is the Guru. But the Guru in Sikhism is no ordinary being. He is divinely inspired. He is attuned to the Supreme Being. He is identified with the Lord in spirit. He is a link. A conduit. The boatman who ferries the devotee across the ocean. Guru Arjan himself was one. Guru Nanak, his master, had reincarnated himself in him as he himself was going to do in his successor, Guru Hargobind. The Guru, in fact, is not the mortal, flesh and blood, but the Divine in him. It is like the Divine in *Shabd*, or *Nam*, the Name. It is also described as *Akshra* in some hymns. *Nam* stands for Divination and Shabd for the Divine utterance. We have the proof of it in Guru Gobind Singh consecrating the *Pothi* at the close of his ministry as the Holy Granth and bequeathing it with the Divine stewardship of the Sikh community. He ordained, "Those who wish to seek the Lord, will find Him in these pages." It was duly recorded and is repeated every morning after the Sikh prayer in the Gurdwaras:

> *As ordained by God, the Lord Eternal,*
> *A new way of life is evolved.*
> *All the Sikhs are asked*
> *To accept the Holy Granth as the Guru.*
> *Guru Granth should be accepted*
> *As the living God.*
> *Those who wish to seek the Lord*
> *Will find Him in the Shabd.*

It is also a fact that in Guru Arjan's hymns and the rest of the Sikh scripture, Rama and several other Hindu Gods are invoked many times. It is maintained that they serve as symbols of the Divine Identity and not the Gods as propitiated in Hinduism. Evidently, Guru Arjan and the other Sikh Gurus had to talk in the idiom of the day with metaphors and similes prevalent in the times. Hence such references, at times, create confusion.

In a society ridden with Islamic overbearance and Brahminic exclusiveness, Guru Nanak brought in a simple creed free from communal bigotry of the Muslims and the ceremonial slavery of the Hindus. And yet it was highly scientific. It inculcated living in the Divine Presence (*Simran*), honest labour (*Kirt Karni*) and sharing it with others (*Wand Chhakna*).

Guru Nanak had laid stress on clean living:

> *Truth is above all*
> *Yet above truth is truthful living.*

Living a truthful life is a reward in itself. However, there is eternal longing in the soul for union with the Absolute. To attain this, what is prescribed is the simple repetition of, and contemplation on the Name. The Name is identical with the Creator. The Name stands for devotion. Says Guru Arjan:

> *All the living creatures are created by the Name.*
> *The Name has brought about planets and spheres.*

THE SUKHMANI

It is advised that one should remember the Name to the extent of its becoming a reflex action (*Ajpa Jaap*). One should repeat the Name without moving the lips physically. Ever so many times Guru Arjan makes exhortations to this effect:

> *Remember the One who prevails over all,*
> *Whose Name is on the countless lips and more.*
> *The Verified Vedas, Puranas and Smrities*
> *Are created by a single syllable of His Name.*
> *Whoever is blessed with an iota of it,*
> *He is beyond all praise.*
>
> THE SUKHMANI

There is no scope for Hath Yoga or other complex Yogic exercises in the Sikh way of life. No rubbing of ashes on the body. No fasting and torturing oneself. No suppression or dissolution. Guru Arjan makes repeated references to it:

> *I read Scriptures and studied the Vedas*
> *Underwent the Yogic discipline of Nival and*
> * Bhoingam.*
> *Yet I could not be rid of the five evils;*
> *Caught I was with conceit and egoism...*
> *Praying for understanding, wisdom and lore*
> *I took to silence, forsook pots and pans,*
> *Naked in the jungle I roamed,*
> *Also the river banks and the temples all over*
> *Yet the mind-set of duality could not be forsworn.*
>
> THE SUKHMANI

Next to the Name is *Shabd* or maybe the Name leads to the *Shabd*. The *Shabd* is the form that the Formless Creator assumes. The *Shabd* is read. The *Shabd* is sung. *Nam* is remembrance. The *Nam* and the Shabd together lead to a state of poise called *Sahaj*. It is an ethico-spiritual stage, a stage of equipoise, illumi-nation. There are no unnatural austerities. No esoteric praxis. Guru Arjan delineates the path of devotion that prescribes no 'forced' practices of self-purification; everything emanates from the higher and the nobler self. And the man arrives and merges with the Divine. In the words of Guru Arjan:

> *He who listens with devotion and bears it in his*
> *   heart,*
> *He is the one who remembers God.*
> *He is relieved from the agony of transmigration.*
> *In an instant his body attains salvation.*
> *A fair name he has and an ambrosial sweet tone,*
> *Who has in his heart the Name of God alone.*
> *Gone are his sorrows, maladies, doubts and*
> *   fright,*
> *Known as the Godman what he does is right.*

THE SUKHMANI

Sri Raga

Sri Raga V, Score I

Absorbed in the spectacle of sons
  and fancy arrays of your spouse,
You enjoy and feel happy
  leading a colourful life.
You ask for more and more and get bloated
  with excesses.
You remember not the Creator,
The blind and conceited wretch that you are. (1)

Man! God alone is the purveyor of peace.
He is realised through the grace of the Guru;
  a gift of one's Karma.
Lost in apparel, gold and silver
  that would be reduced to dust,
Varieties of horses and elephants
  and untiring chariots;
None you give quarter,
  ignoring even the near and dear ones.
You have forgotten your Creator
  without whose Name you remain unclean. (2)

Amassing wealth you invite curses.
All that you cherish is evanescent like you.
Following the dictates of your conceit,
  you indulge in ego.
He who forgets God, he has neither status nor
  honour. (3)

The True Guru has introduced me to the One
  who is the lone Friend.
He is the protector of the devotee,
  the mortals cry in ego in vain.
God does what the devotee desires.
None ever returns empty-handed from His door.
He finds the world enlightened,
Nanak is dyed in His colour. (4)

(42)

Sri Raga V

If you were to cultivate Him alone,
  you would acquire everything else.
If you repeat His True Name,
  your objective of life is achieved.
He who has inscribed on his forehead,
  he arrives at the Lord's Court.
Man! Devote yourself to Him alone.
Without Him the rest is the false lure of
  Maya. (1)

If the True Guru is gracious,
  one enjoys a million pleasures and kingly
  powers.

With a mite of His Name,
  my mind and body are satiate.
He who has written in his lot,
  The Master's feet he propitiates. (2)

He who loves the True One,
  his hours and moments are blessed.
He who has God's Name as his support,
  he suffers neither anguish nor agony.
He alone is ferried across,
  whom the Guru gives His hand. (3)

The spot where the saints meet is pleasant and
  sacred.
They are vindicated who find the True
  Preceptor.
Nanak has arrived at the stage
  where there is no death, no ageing, nor any
  birth ever. (4)

(44)

Sri Raga V

Man! Remember the One who is the King of
  kings.
Depend upon Him alone,
  whom everyone seeks for succour.
Forsaking all the clever ways,
  seek a seat at the Guru's feet. (1)

Man! Meditate on the Name in peace and poise.
Remember Him day and night and sing His
  praises.

Man! Fall at His feet who has not the like of
  Him.
Remembering whom brings utmost peace
  without any malady and pain whatsoever.
Serve the Lord ever, He is the True Master. (2)

In the company of the Holy one gets purified
  and escapes the stranglehold of Yama.
Pray to Him who brings comfort and drives
  away fear.
When the Benevolent Lord is gracious
  everything falls in place. (3)

However high we may describe Him,
  He is higher than the highest.
He is beyond (the description) of colours and
  features,
He cannot be assessed.
Pray God! do be gracious
  with True Name let Nanak be blessed. (4)

                                                    (44)

Sri Raga V, Score 2

The cowherd has come to the pasture,
  Why beat the drum?
When the time is over go you must
  winding up your affairs.
Man! Sing God's praises
  and serve the True Guru with devotion.
Why must you feel elated for matters small? (1)

Like the overnight guest, you have to depart
  early in the morning.
Involved in the family affairs
  which are only like a flower bed. (2)

What for the passion for possession?
  Seek the One who gives.
In the end you have to quit
  leaving behind the millions and billions. (3)

Wandering about the eighty-four lakh births
  you've obtained the difficult-to-obtain life.
Says Nanak, be prepared, your day is close
  by. (4)

(50)

Sri Raga V

As long as you are with your spouse,
  you live a delightful life.
The moment the spouse departs,
  In the dust you find resort. (1)

My heart misses Him, I long for His glimpse.
Blessed is His seat.
As long as the spouse is at home, everybody
  adores the Master.
The moment the spouse departs,
  nobody would give quarter. (2)

She who serves the spouse at her parents'
  she lives happily at the in-laws.

She who learns the art of life from the Guru,
  she never comes to grief. (3)

All have to consummate the marriage;
  all have to go to the in-laws.
Says Nanak, blessed is the happily-married
  who is devoted to her Lord. (4)

                              (50–51)

Sri Raga, Score 7

Depending upon Your indulgence,
  I whiled away my time in filial love.
I am an erring child,
You are the gracious parent.
It's easy to boast but difficult to belong to You. (1)

You are my pride; You are my power.
To You I come.
You are amidst us; You are outside us. (2)

Father! I know not Your ways.
You are the deliverer of Your devotees.
You must protect me, my Lord ! (3)

I found salvation with the grace of God.
Meeting the Guru has led Nanak to know the
  Lord. (4)

                              (51–52)

Sri Raga V

He who is in trouble,
Without support from any quarter,
Who is chased by foes,
   the friends too desert him.
Whose all succour vanishes
   with no help coming from anywhere,
Were he to contemplate on God,
   no gust of hot wind would sear him. (1)

He is the support of the supportless.
He comes not nor does He go.
He is Eternal, Immutable.
One learns this truth through the Divine Word.
He who is feeble, afflicted with destitution and
   hunger,
Not a pice in his pocket, sans any solace.
He who cannot help himself
   and is without any achievement to his credit,
Were he to contemplate on God,
   everlasting his rule would be. (2)

He who has worries galore,
   suffers many a malady.
Engrossed in the affairs of his family;
   at times happy, at others unhappy,
Wandering the world over,
   resting not for a moment.
Were he to contemplate on God,
   his mind and body would be at peace. (3)

He who is addicted to lust, wrath and
  attachment, a miser given to greed,
Perpetrator of the four cardinal sins,
  a demon who is wasting away,
He who lends his ears not to the Scriptures,
  the Holy melody and song,
Were he to contemplate on God;
  a moment's remembrance and he'll be cruised
  across. (4)

You may recite the Shastras, Smrities and the
  four Vedas.
You may practise penance like the Yogis and go
  on pilgrimage.
You may perform the six rituals or twice their
  number and engage in worship after bath.
But without devotion to God
  you will inevitably come to loss. (5)

He who wields power, owns estate, is well
  connected and enjoys life in full,
He who has attractive gardens,
  whose writ of an egotist runs,
He who has a lot of fun
  in a variety of ways to engage him,
If he doesn't contemplate on the Supreme Lord,
  he is condemned to be a serpent born. (6)

If he is much rich, lives well
  and has a clean reputation,
He has loving parents,
  sons, brothers and friends,

He has a lashkar with armoured soldiers,
  owing their allegiance to him.
If he remember not the Supreme Lord well,
  he will be consigned to the lowest hell. (7)

He who has no physical ailment or deformity,
  no anxiety and no sorrow,
Who cares not for death
  and is lost merry-making day and night,
Goes on amassing wealth without scruples,
If he doesn't remember the Supreme Lord,
  he'll find himself in the Yama's ward. (8)

If God is gracious, one acquires company of
  the Holy.
The more one cultivates it,
  the more one gains the vision of the Divine.
He is the Master of both this world and the
  next; there is no other place.
Nanak gained the True Name with the Guru's
  grace. (9)

(70–71)

Sri Raga V, Score 5

I know not what pleases Him.
I am on the road in quest.
The mystic meditates.
The scholar ruminates.
Few have found the Lord. (1)

The Vaishnav observes discipline.
The Yogi believes in none.
The ascetic is lost in asceticism. (2)

The silence-vower would speak not.
One is a recluse.
The other is a man of family.
The anchorite is given to anchoritism. (3)

There are practitioners of the nine orders.
While the learned advocates the Vedas.
The house-holder is engrossed in the house-hold
  affairs. (4)

There are slogan-mongers.
Also those given to disguising themselves.
And they who remain naked.
The ones peculiarly clad.
And those who recite and entertain.
Many who practise vigil.
Some bathe at places of pilgrimage. (5)

Others who fast.
And the practitioners of untouchability.
Some go underground and would not be seen,
While others are given to quiet contemplation. (6)

Nobody denies it;
All claim to have realised Him.
He alone is devotee whom He unites. (7)

Giving up questioning
Nanak comes to His protection.
At the Guru's feet he finds satisfaction. (8)

(71)

Sri Raga V

Sitting at His feet, I adore Him.
The True Guru has brought about this meeting.
There is none as grand as He is.
My Master is loving;
Sweeter than mother and father,
Brothers, sisters and friends;
  there is none like Him. (1)

Comes the month of Sawan, as per His
  command
I ply the plough of Truth,
Sow the seeds of the Name hopefully,
And with His grace I gather a plentiful crop. (2)

***   ***   .   ***

I am my Master's champion wrestler.
Because of Him I have this high status.
All the spectators have assembled.
The Creator too has come to watch. (17)

The wind and percussion instruments are
  played.
The wrestlers have landed in the ring.
I vanquished the five combatants
  and my Guru patted me on the back. (18)

While coming everyone was alike;
Returning home they change their complexion.
The Guru-conscious earn profit,
While the egotist lose the capital too. (19)

He is beyond colour and complexion.
He is seen present everywhere in person.
They hear His Name and sing His praises,
The devotees of the Mine of Virtues. (20)

I've served the Lord from time immemorial.
The Guru snapped my bonds of captivity.
No more do have I again to play.
Nanak availed of the chance that came his
    way. (21)

(73–74)

Sri Raga V

In the first quarter of the night, my merchant
    friend! You were implanted in the womb.
Ten months to be born, my merchant friend!
    Avail of an opportunity to meditate on Him.
The opportunity to meditate on Him
    is as per command of the Highest Court.
The attachment obtaining in the mother, father,
    brother, son and wife is a gift of God.
Good and bad deeds are also ordained by Him,
    man can do nothing on his own.
Says Nanak, the first quarter is the time
    when one is conceived in the womb. (1)

In the second quarter of the night, my merchant
friend! Your youth is in high tide.
Your mind lost in conceit,
you distinguish not between good and bad.
Distinguish you not between good and bad,
it's an arduous path ahead.
You've never served the True Guru
while the Yama waits, over your head, my
merchant friend!
What will be your defence
when the Dharamraja arraigns you?
Says Nanak, during the second quarter
the tide of youth is high. (2)

In the third quarter of night, my merchant
friend! You garner poison in blind ignorance.
Embroiled in the love of wife and progeny, my
merchant friend!
You are caught in the gale of avarice.
Caught in the gale of avarice
O man, you remember not God.
Having not sought the company of the Holy
you suffer many an incarnation.
You forgot the Creator
and contemplated not on the Master for a
moment.
Says Nanak, in the third quarter
man garners poison in blind ignorance. (3)

In the fourth quarter of the night, my merchant
friend!
Your day (of departure) has drawn close.

Contemplate on the Name with the devout, my
    merchant friend!
Which will be your help in the Final Court.
Contemplate on the Name with the
    devoute, man!
Who will assist you in the end.
The love of Maya will serve you not,
    the false attachment you have developed.
All your night is lost in ignorance,
    for light you must serve the True Guru.
Says Nanak, it is the fourth quarter, man
    your day (of departure) has drawn close. (4)

As the writ of the Lord arrives, my merchant
    friend!
You have to proceed with whatever you have
    gained.
They will not allow you a moment's respite,
    they will hold you fast.
They carry you as per the orders,
    the egotists are ever in trouble.
Those who serve the Perfect Guru,
    they are happy in the Supreme Court.
The body is the soil in this world,
    you reap what you sow.
Says Nanak, the devotees are welcome in the
    High Court,
While the conceited have from place to place
    go. (5)

(77–78)

Sri Raga V

There is but One God.
He is realised through the grace of the True
Guru.

Dear my friend! Do remember God's Name.
Dear . my friend! He alone abides by you.
Meditating on Him, not a moment goes waste
in His company.
He who meditates at His lotus-feet
reaps the desired fruit.
God prevails on earth and ocean
and takes kindly to each one of us.
Nanak advises you, dear friend!
Company of the Holy helps remove doubts. (1)

Dear my friend! Besides God the rest is all a
myth.
Dear my friend! It is poison the ocean that the
world is.
Adopting His lotus-feet as your boat,
the disease of doubt will not afflict you.
He is fortunate who cultivates the Perfect Guru
and contemplates on God all the while.
From time immemorial He takes care of those
who serve Him;
The devotees have His Name as their support.
Nanak advises you, dear friend!
Besides God everything else is mere myth. (2)

Dear my friend! Imbibing God is a good
  bargain.
Dear my friend! You occupy His Eternal Portal.
He who serves Him and imbibes the mystery,
  attains a permanent seat.
Neither He takes birth nor He dies.
He is free from the affliction of doubt.
The account of Chitragupta is annulled,
  the Yama becomes helpless.
Nanak advises you dear friend! Imbibing God is
  a good bargain. (3)

Dear my friend! You should cultivate the Holy.
Dear my friend! Contemplate on the Name for
  enlightenment.
Contemplate on the Master who is easily
  accessible and fulfills all your wishes.
The good deeds done earlier, take you to God
  who unites the long-separated.
He prevails inside and outside, my mind is
  convinced.
Nanak advises dear friend! You should cultivate
  the Holy. (4)

Dear my friend! Dedicate yourself to the loving
  devotion of God.
Dear my friend! The way fish loves water.
Sipping the Amrit of Divine Word
  you will enjoy all the comforts.
You'll attain God, sing the songs of joy.
With the grace of God your desires will be
  met.

He will take you over, bless you with Nine
   Treasures,
And grant you the Name in abandon.
Nanak advises the Sikh and the saint,
   dedicate yourself to Him in loving devotion. (5)

(79–80)

Raga Majh

Raga Majh V, Quartet Score 1

I long to see my Guru.
My heart wails like Chatrik.
Without a sight of the dear Sage
  my thirst is not slaked, I feel not quenched.
I am sacrifice unto a glimpse
  of my dear Guru, my Godman. (1)

Yours is a charming face.
Your words, a Divine melody.
For long I haven't seen my Lord.
Blessed is the land where You live
  my well-wisher, my friend, my God!
I am sacrifice unto my well-wishers, my friend,
  my God! (2)

It was (a torture of) Kaliyug
  if I didn't see You for a moment.
When do I see you now, my beloved Lord?
My night knows no end,
I have lost my sleep,
  without visiting the Guru's Darbar.
I am sacrifice unto the Darbar of my Guru. (3)

It was a blessing meeting the Saint-Guru.
I found the God Eternal in my own house.
Let me serve Him without a moment's respite,
Nanak, the slave has this claim.
I am sacrifice unto Him Whose servant I
  remain. (4)

(97)

Majh V

Blessed is the season in which I remember You.
Blessed is the endeavour in Your pursuit.
Blessed is the heart in which You dwell.
You who are the Master of us all. (1)

Father! You are the True Lord.
Endless are Your Nine Treasures.
He is content to whom You give.
He becomes Your devotee. (2)

Everyone looks up to You.
You dwell in every heart.
All are equal in Your eyes;
No one is a stranger to You. (3)

You grant salvation to men of God.
The egoist is born again and again.
Says Nanak, I am sacrifice unto You,
All that I witness is Your creation. (4)

(97)

Majh V

The home that bristles with conjugal bliss,
  resounds with joyous melodies.
Dance and drama behove the home
  where the wife is adored by her spouse. (1)

She who is loved by her spouse is virtuous and
  lucky.
Progeny-blessed, suave and happily-married,
Charming, efficient and clever. (2)

The one who is dedicated to the loving
  devotion of the spouse,
She is highly cultured, pre-eminent,
Richly equipped with learning,
Of noble lineage and several brothers. (3)

No words can praise her,
She who has been accepted by her spouse.
Eternal is her conjugal bliss
With the Unreached and Unknowable God.
Says Nanak, she owes her loving devotion to
  the Lord. (4)

(97–98)

Majh V

It's agony when He is remembered not.
His longing makes me roam a lot.
Meditating on the Name is joy forever,
For him who is blessed by the Merciful
  Lord. (1)

My True Guru is all-powerful,
  my sorrows vanish as I remember Him.
Gone are worries, maladies and pain,
  Himself He takes care of me. (2)

Like a child I ask for everything.
There is no end to His mercy.
Falling at His feet I adore my God. (3)

I am sacrifice unto my Perfect Lord.
He Who has broken all my bonds,
With His Name He has cleansed my heart.
Nanak is lost in His colourful mart. (4)

(98)

Majh V

You are the reservoir of water,
  I am Your fish.
Your Name is the drop,
  I am the thirsty Chatrik.
You are my hope, I cherish You,
  On You alone my mind is set. (1)

The way a baby enjoys sucking milk,
The way the poor is pleased with the sight of
  wealth,
The thirsty drink the water chilled,
With God's Name my heart is full. (2)

Like the candle flushing darkness with light.
The thought of the groom delights the bride.

The way meeting with the lover lends fervour,
My heart is dyed in the Lord's colour. (3)

The Godman has put me on the Divine path,
With the grace of the Holy, I've taken to the sort.
God is mine; I am God's slave,
The truth His Guru to Nanak gave. (4)

(100)

Majh V

Your word is like Amrit,
Hearing which I am liberated.
Anxieties gone, my mind is at peace
With the glimpse of the Guru True. (1)

I am happy; sorrow having fled away,
As I heard the Name from the lips of the Holy.
All the tanks are full to the brim,
  None has remained unfilled. (2)

The Creator Himself has been merciful.
He takes care of all the creation.
Kind, Benevolent and Charitable,
  He satisfies all the needy. (3)

Infusing life in the forests and green of the
    Universe;
The Creator did it in a moment.
Nanak, the Guru-conscious remembers Him
  Whom He Has His ear lent. (4)

(103)

Majh V

You are my father.
You are my mother.
You are my relative,
And my brother.
You are my saviour everywhere.
I have neither worry nor fear. (1)

Blessed by You, I come to know You.
You are my anchor.
You are my pride.
There is none other than You.
It's all Your play, this world, my Beau! (2)

Everything living is Your Creation.
You make them do what You please.
Whatever happens is ordained by You.
None other has anything with it to do. (3)

I gained the precious peace remembering Your
   Name.
Singing God's praises
I am contented at heart.
With the grace of the Guru,
I have succeeded in the perilous task. (4)

(104)

Majh V

Where the Name of the Merciful Lord is
   repeated,
The deserted mansions get gilded.

Where God's Name is not remembered,
The towns are wrecked and ruined. (1)

He who contemplates on God on frugal fare,
God takes care of him both here and there.
He who overeats and indulges in misdeeds,
Raises a crop of poisonous weeds. (2)

He who doesn't cultivate the Holy,
In the company of the misled he commits folly.
The ignorant ruins the precious life,
    he himself uproots his own tribe. (3)

I seek Your support, my Lord Benevolent!
The ocean of solace, my Guru Omniscient!
Do be kind that I sing Your praises,
Let Nanak's faith receive no dent. (4)

(105)

Barah Mah
(Song of the Twelve Months)

Majh V

There is but one God,
He is realised through the grace of the True
  Guru.

Distanced because of my deeds and Karma,
Lord God! be gracious and bridge this gap.
I've gone round the four quarters
And ten directions,
Tired, I now turn to You for refuge.
The cow gone dry is of little use.
Without water the crop withers and fetches no
  price.
In the absence of the spouse how can the
  bride be at peace?
A house without the spouse
Is like a deserted village, an accursed town.
What use is dressing up lavishly,
Munching betel and comely figure?
With the Lord God not being there,
The associates and friends look like doom.

*Prays Nanak, O Lord! bless me with Your
    Name as gift.
And let me meet the Master
Whose is this imperishable domain.* (1)

*In the month of Chet to enjoy life in full,
    meditate on God.
Repeat His Name with your tongue in the
    company of the Holy.
Those who are united with the Lord,
Their visit is worth it.
Living without Him even for a moment
Is a breath gone waste.
He who prevails on land and sea
And is found in forests,
Remembering not such a Lord
What agony must it be!
Blessed manifold are they
Who are devoted to such a God.
I long to have a glimpse of my Master,
Nanak thirsts for Him.
In the month of Chet I propitiate His feet
Who takes me to my Lord Supreme.* (2)

*He who suffers separation in the month of
    Baisakh,
How can he have peace of mind?
Forgetting the Benevolent Lord,
He takes to the lure of Maya.
Excepting the Lord Eternal
Neither sons, nor wife, nor wealth will
    accompany him.*

Many have perished clinging to them,
False attachments as they are.
Without imbibing the Name of God
He will be lost hereafter.
Disregarding the Divine, one must suffer;
There is no other (protection) than the Lord.
Those who opt for God's care,
They are talked well of.
Nanak longs to be with His Person of glory.
Baisakh is pleasant for those who adore God
In the company of the Holy. (3)

In the month of Jeth adore Him whom
    everyone pays obeisance.
Tying yourself to His apron string,
No harm will ever come to you.
His Name is like gems and jewels,
None dare rob them.
All the pleasant colours around
Are His colours.
Do what God bids you to do,
Blessed are those who heed His command.
Whatever He does, they solemnly accept.
Those who are united by Him,
They wail not in separation.
Those who acquire the company of the   Holy,
They are to joy wed.
Jeth is colourful for the blessed
Who has good luck recorded on his forehead. (4)

Asadh scorches those who love not God.
Forsaking the Sustainer of the Universe

Who look upon the mortals for support.
Caught in duality, they have the noose of death
  in their neck.
They reap what they sow,
Whatever is inscribed on their forehead.
The night (of life) having waxed,
They repent as they repair in despair.
Those who cultivate the Holy
They are liberated at the Portals of the Divine.
Pray be kind to me,
I long to have a glimpse of You.
I have none other than God,
This is Nanak's plea.
He enjoys Asadh to his heart's content
Who conjures himself at the feet of the Deity. (5)

Pleased in Sawan is she
Who is devoted to the lotus-feet of the Lord.
Her mind and body are dyed in truth,
Her anchor being the Name of God.
Fake are the hues of temptation
Which she treats as dust.
She is exhilarated with the drop of Amrit
That she sips in the company of the Holy.
With His grace forests and vines are in
  blossom;
He is all-powerful and without any limits.
I long to meet my Lord;
Only Karma can make me do it.
The friends who have gained access to the
  Lord
I am sacrifice unto them.

Lord! Be merciful to Nanak,
Your Word does always tame.
Sawan is the delight of the happily-married
Whose heart is the abode of the Name. (6)

She who is misled by doubts in Bhadon,
And is involved with someone else.
She may dress herself lavishly,
It is all of little use.
The moment she dies, she will be termed a
    ghost.
To an undisclosed destination
The emissaries of death will lead her.
They quit in a moment
All those who had been endeared.
The hands are twisted and the body torn,
The colour turns white from black.
As one sows, so does one reap,
It is the crop of Karma.
Nanak comes to the refuge of the Lord
Whose feet are like a ship (to cruise across).
In Bhadon they are not thrown in Hell
Who have their saviour in Lord God. (7)

I am beside myself with passion in Assu,
How do I go and meet my love?
My mind and body thirst for His glimpse,
Come someone and help me join Him.
The Holy always help the love-lorn,
I prostrate at their feet.
How can one have peace without the Lord?
There is no other place where I can go.

Those who have tasted the essence of love,
Their thirst slaked, they are fully quenched.
They forsake conceit and humbly pray
To be tied to the Lord's apron.
Those who are united with the spouse,
They know not pangs of separation.
There is none other than the Lord God,
Nanak has sought His support.
In Assu they are happy,
Whose kindly God is their forte. (8)

In Kartik one suffers the consequences of one's
   Karma.
Let one not accuse the other.
Forgetting the Lord God,
One is afflicted with many a malady.
Turning away from the Divine
Is like alienating oneself for several births.
In a moment all the rich dainties
Turn bitter in taste.
None can help mediate,
It is no use making daily plaints.
One can do nothing on one's own
Whatever has been ordained (must take place).
Lucky I'll be if I encounter my Lord,
All my woes will be lost.
Do protect Nanak, my Lord
The Breaker of the Bonds of slaves.
In Kartik if you find the company of the Holy,
All your fears are allayed. (9)

In Maghar they look comely
Who have their spouses for their company.
Their praise is beyond words
Who have been united with the Master.
Brought about by the company of the Holy
Their union with the Divine finds them in
   bloom.
Those who remain away from the Holy,
They are left alone.
There is no end to their woes,
They suffer the stranglehold of death.
Those who remember their Lord,
They enjoy His presence ever.
They have God's Name as gems, jewels and
   diamonds
Woven around their necks.
Nanak seeks the dust (of their feet),
Who seek God's support at His Gate.
In Maghar if you remember God
Transmigration is no more your fate. (10)

In Pokh they suffer not cold
Who are close to the bosom of their Lord God.
Their mind fixed at His feet
They are blessed with the presence of the
   Master.
They have the support of Gobind and Gopal
And the advantage of His service.
They are afflicted not with evil.
They sing His praises in the company of the
   Holy.

They merge into from where they emerged;
It is the reward of true love.
God stretched His hand and pulled them out,
Not to be separated again.
I am sacrifice unto Him a million times,
My True Friend, Inaccessible and Unknowable.
Finding Nanak at His Portal
The Lord God felt amused.
Pokh is pleasant to him with its comforts
Who has been by Lord excused. (11)

In the month of Magh take your ceremonial
  bath
In the dust of the feet of the Holy.
Listen and repeat the Name of God
And share it with others.
It will wash the filth of life's Karma
And help shed the conceit of the mind.
Lust and anger will no more afflict you,
You will also be relieved of the dog of avarice.
Treading the truthful path,
The entire world will hail you.
Taking pity on the fellow-beings
Is like bathing at sixty-eight places of
  pilgrimage.
He is fortunate
Whom He blesses in His mercy.
Nanak is sacrifice unto them
Who have accomplished the Divine.
They are considered clean in Magh
Who are favoured by the Guru kind. (12)

There is a lot of fun in Phagun.
God reveals Himself in (this month).
The Godmen who are the lieutenants of the Lord
Bring about the union in their grace.
The bed is bedecked with every comfort,
There is no room any more for sorrow.
The fortunate have all their desires fulfilled,
They find their spouse in the Lord God.
The friends sing songs in chorus
In praise of the Divine.
There is none other like God,
None else can match Him.
He betters one's lot here and hereafter.
And allots a permanent seat.
Saves in the ocean of the world,
One does not have to be born again.
He has countless virtues while I have a single
    tongue.
Nanak who sought His support is ferried
    across.
One must adore God in Phagun,
Who has none of His own needs to ask. (13)

Those who meditate on the Name,
Have their jobs done.
Those who remember the Perfect Guru,
Are found truthful at the Heavenly Portals.
God's feet are a seat of comfort,
To ferry across the turbulent ocean.
Those who are smitten with the loving devotion,
Burn not in the flames of evil.
Forsaking untruth and duality

They are replete with truth.
They serve the Lord God
With Him alone in the heart.
Their months and days are auspicious
To whom He does the favour.
Nanak supplicates just for a glimpse,
God! Do be gracious, my Saviour. (14)

(133–36)

Raga Gauri

Gauri, Guareri Quartet

There is but One God.
He is realised through the grace of the True
  Guru.

How do I gain felicity, my brother?
How do I acquire the Name as support? (1)

Because of Maya, I have no happiness at home,
With lofty mansions of alluring appearance.
In false greed I've lost my life.
Content at the sight of elephants and steeds,
Lashkars around with lieutenants and the elite;
They are a mere noose of ego in the neck. (2)

He who rules over all the ten directions
And enjoys the company of many women,
Is like the king who finds himself a beggar in
  the dream. (3)

My True Guru has shown me the way to
  felicity.
The devotee of God accepts what He does.
Nanak, the slave killed his ego and in God is
  absorbed. (4)

This is how you gain felicity.
This is how you acquire the Name as support
  from the Deity

(175–176)

Gauri Guareri V

For many a birth you were worm and insect.
For many a birth elephant, fish and deer.
For many a birth you were bird and serpent.
For many a birth yoked as horse and bullock. (1)

Adore the Creator, here is an opportunity.
You've found this life after an eternity.
For many a birth you were rock and mountain.
For many a birth you were born a human.
For many a birth you were made into twigs.
Eighty-four lakh births you have had to
  wander. (2)

Cultivate the Holy in the current strife.
Serve the godly and remember the Giver of
  life.
Forsake your ego and false conceit.
He who dies in life is accepted in the Divine

Retreat. (3)

Whatever is to be done, you alone can do.
None else can undertake it for you.
You meet only when the Master deigns.
Nanak adores Him even in chain. (4)

(176)

Gauri Guareri V

He who raised you from clay to a jewel,
Sustained you in the womb with utmost care,
Who gave you good name and glory,
You must remember Him day and night.
Lord! If I am granted dust of a Godman's feet,
In the company of the Guru, I'll remember my
    Master. (1)

He who turned the ignorant in me to be
    eloquent,
From the senseless to the sensible one,
On whose account I gained the Nine Treasures,
I must not forget such a Master. (2)

He who gave shelter to the shelterless,
He who gave honour to the one without
    honour,
He who gave me whatever I like,
Remember Him with every breath day and
    night. (3)

At whose behest the bond of Maya is severed,

*With the Guru's grace the poison to Amrit is
   turned.*
*Says Nanak, nothing happens by man's
   endeavour.*
You must adore Him who is the Saviour. (4)

(177)

Gauri Guareri V

Man believes, this body is his.
Again and again he clings to it.
Sons and spouse, he is lost in the family,
Who wouldn't let him serve the Deity. (1)

How does one adore the Lord?
How does one the Maya discard?
What is good he treats as untoward.
What is truth he considers false.
*Knows not the difference between victor and
   the vanquished.*
This is the way of the misled in the world. (2)

What is poison the stupid would drink.
The Name ambrosial he treats as bitter.
He is never close to the men of God.
Keeps on moving the eighty-four lakh jaunt. (3)

All the birds are caught in the net.
They cherish it in various ways as best.
Says Nanak, the one of whom He is fond,
The Perfect Guru snaps his bonds. (4)

(180)

Gauri Guareri V

If You please, I'm in the right frame.
If God is gracious I remember His Name.
If God is gracious the worldly bonds snap.
If You are gracious, I live not in the ego's lap.
If You please, I serve You.
On my own it is nothing I can do. (1)

If You so desire, I recite the Scripture.
If You so desire, Truth becomes my elixir.
If You so desire, the True Guru is kind.
Your grace and all the comfort I find. (2)

He whom You please, does good deeds.
He whom You please, Truth becomes his creed.
The treasure of virtues belongs to you.
You are the Master whom the prayers are
  due. (3)

God's love purifies both mind and body.
All the cheer lies in the Holy company.
I long alone for devotion to Your Name.
For Nanak Salvation is his ultimate aim. (4)

(180)

Gauri Guareri V

You are my companion, You are my confidant.
You are my love, with You I am bound.
You are my honour and my embellishment.
Without You I can live not for a moment.

You are my darling, my breath, my relief.
You are my Master, You are my Chief. (1)

I live the way You ordain.
I live the way You explain.
Wherever I see it is You I claim.
Fearless my tongue repeats Your Name. (2)

You are my nine precious treasures.
Provider of my life, source of my pleasure.
You are my succour, You are my pride.
You are my sustenance, You are my guide. (3)

I remember You in my body and mind.
The secret I have learnt from my Guru kind.
The True Guru wrought me in this mould.
Nanak has God alone as his support. (4)

(181)

Raga Gauri Guareri
Quartets and Couplets

There is but One God.
He is realised through the grace of the True
  Guru.

What belongs to others, you try to claim.
What you must abandon, you wish to attain.
How on earth could you meet the Lord?
You long for what is forbidden by God. (1)

You accept as true, what is untrue.
And what is true you would not pursue. (2)

You walk on the left with misled throng.
Deviating from the right, your weave is
  wrong. (3)

God Himself is the Master of both ways.
He whom He blesses, says Nanak, is saved. (4)

                                            (185)

Gauri V

He who has God as his friend,
He doesn't need anyone else.
He who has endeared himself to the Lord,
All his fears and dreads are shed. (1)

He who enjoys remembering Him,
He does not enjoy anything else. (2)

He who is received in His Court,
He cares for none other than Him (3)

He who submits himself to the Deity,
Says Nanak, he is ever and ever happy. (4)

Gauri V

The lucky one! It is a rare incarnation, you've
  attained.
It is committing suicide if you remember not
  His Name.
Those who forget Him, they must die.
Without His Name what use is life? (1)

Eating, drinking, playing and laughing galore,
What good for those who have to live no
*   more?* (2)

He who sings not the praises of the Master
*   Divine,*
He is worse than the beasts, birds and the
*   kind.* (3)

Nanak's Guru has shown him the path;
His Name alone he repeats in his heart. (4)

                                                    (188)

Gauri V

The big you see around
Are afflicted with anguish, anxieties and fears.
No one is big being rich, (it's a whim).
He is big who remembers Him. (1)

The landlord keeps on clamouring for land;
He rests not until runs out the sand. (2)

Nanak has known a secret,
Without God's Name,
*   there is no rest.* (3)

                                                    (188)

Gauri V

With the Guru's grace, I imbibed the Name.
And thus could the restless mind tame.

Singing His praises I was at peace;
My sorrows gone, the struggle ceased. (1)

Remembering the lotus-feet of the Seer,
All my worries seem to disappear. (2)

Forsaking all, the helpless sought His support;
Thus he qualified for a seat in His Court. (3)

All his pains, sufferings, doubts and fears
  vanished.
When the Creator in Nanak's heart settled. (4)

(189)

Gauri V

He to whom He is kind.
He would keep Him ever in mind.
Forgetting Him one suffers the torture of
  duality;
Remembering the Name, doubts and fear are a
  casualty. (1)

He who hears and sings His praises,
No sorrow ever towards him gazes. (2)

Serving God is Man's glory.
The evil of Maya is no more his worry. (3)

Remembering the kind God with his tongue and
  mind,
Nanak is freed from entanglements of every
  kind. (4)

(190)

Gauri V

I was redeemed by the great Guru.
The conceited lives ever to rue.
Dear friend! you must to the Guru yourself
devote.
So that you are felicitated in His Court. (1)

Contemplating at the Guru's feet,
Your sorrows, fears and misfortunes will
retreat. (2)

The Guru's word will be ever by your side,
Everyone else with you will abide. (3)

When Guru the great took kindly to me,
Says Nanak, I was only then redeemed. (4)

(191)

Gauri V

In an instant He turned green the dry.
With His ambrosial glance He infused new life.
The great Guru kindly terminated tribulations.
And the worker given work in His own
fashion. (1)

The desires met, the worries were behind.
The Treasure of Virtue, the Guru was kind. (2)

Sorrows were over and joys landed,
Not a moment's delay when the Guru
commanded. (3)

He found the great Guru, his longings met.
Says Nanak, such a one is ever a success. (4)

(191)

Gauri V

No more distress; God has brought peace.
It is all quiet, the Lord is pleased.
I am happy with the grace of God.
Distanced for ages, I have been united by the
* Lord.* (1)

Remembering the Name of the Seer,
All the maladies have come to disappear. (2)

Reciting the Scriptures in His quest,
Repeating His Name with every breath, (3)

Sorrow, pain and Yama would never haunt,
Says Nanak, he who God's praises chants. (4)

(191)

Gauri V

If You so please, Your Name I repeat.
At the Divine Portal I find a seat.
There is none other than You, my Lord!
Your blessings and all my problems are solved. (1)
Remembering You Master, no malady afflicts.
Doubts and fears with Your Name quit. (2)

You are the Supreme, the Limitless Lord.
Aware of what is there in every heart. (3)

I supplicate my kindly Guru,
To bless Nanak with the Name True. (4)

(192)

Gauri V

God's devotee and the non-believer don't go
together.
One is given to evil ways, dyed in Divine
colour is the other.
The way one acquainted with the know-how
alone, cannot a caparisoned horse ride,
The way a hermaphrodite cannot make love to
a bride. (1)

Trying to milk a bull tied with spencel
Chasing a lion riding a kine damsel, (2)

Worshipping sheep like a Kamdhenu,*
Going out for shopping without money! (3)

Says Nanak, contemplate on the Name Divine.
Remember the Master like a friend sublime. (4)

(198)

Gauri V

Do only that what soils not yourself.
In the adoration of God should your mind ever
dwell.

---

* A wish-fulfilling mythical cow.

Remember the One forsaking duality.
Repeat His Name in the company of the
   Holy. (1)

Ritual, Dharma, fasts and prayers,
Other than God you must not care. (2)

His labours alone the fruits bear,
Who is devoted to the Master dear. (3)

Among the followers of Vishnu, he is supreme,
Says Nanak, who sheds the manners mean. (4)

(199)

Gauri V

He who shouts at the poor
Comes to grief.
God does justice;
He looks after His devotee. (1)

He is adored from the Primal Hour to Eternity.
He who decries Him
Dies a wretched death. (2)

He kills himself,
No one may save him.
He is talked ill of
Here and hereafter. (3)

God saves His servants,
Holding them to His heart.

Says Nanak, submit yourself to Him
And meditate on His Word. (4)

(199)

Gauri V

I am at peace.
The Guru has bestowed peace.
I am free from pain and sin.
Daily I repeat the Name of God.
All my ills have disappeared. (1)

I have gained Salvation in the company of the
  Holy.
God's greatness is unfathomable. (2)

It is in God's company that one finds
  deliverance.
I sing praises of the Blemishless every day.
My afflictions are gone and I am saved. (3)

I remember God in word and thought.
Says Nanak, His protection I have got. (4)

(200)

Gauri V

O Godmen! Know this for certain in your
  mind,
The True One solves all your problems.
He defeats all your sworn enemies.
He saves the honour of His devotees. (1)

Kings and kings' kings are all under His sway.
He drinks the great drink of Nectar. (2)

Remembering His Name I shed my fears.
In the company of Godmen I surrendered my
 lot. (3)

I fell at the feet of the Omniscient.
His protection alone Nanak has sought. (4)

(201)

Gauri Purbi V

There is but One God.
He is realised through the grace of the True
 Guru.

Mother! How do I meet my life's Sustainer?
I have neither looks, nor   wits, nor strength, (1)

Coming from afar, I am a stranger.
I have neither money nor with youth incensed.
Do take my care, I am ill-fated. (2)

I have turned a recluse in His search,
For His glimpse I wander in thirst. (3)

The Benevolent Lord to the helpless has been
 kind.
Assuaged in the company of the Holy does
 Nanak himself find. (4)

(204)

Gauri V

Awakened in me is the longing for the Lord.
I fall at His feet in a prayerful stance.
If a happy chance brings me to a man of
  God,
I'll dedicate myself and my wealth, shedding
  all my conceit.
He who talks to me about my Lord,
Day and night his company I seek. (1)

When the seed of Karma comes to blossom,
I adore the One who both cherishes and
  forsakes.
Darkness dispels, Nanak meets his Master
After many an age as he wakes. (2)

(204)

Gauri V

Day and night the life shortens;
I do my job under the Guru's guidance.
My cherished friend, I pray to you,
It is my hour to serve the Guru.
If I earn here and leave with gain,
In the next life, I'll be free from pain. (1)

This world is lost in meaningless doubts,
Only a savant can ferry across his boat.
He whom He awakens for the Divine droughts,
He alone perceives His unexpressed
  thoughts. (2)

With the Guru in your mind
Serve the One from where you came.
You'll find felicity at home
And come not back once again. (3)

Knower of my mind, my Creator,
Pray fulfil just one desire of my heart.
Nanak asks for a single treat,
Let him be the dust of the Godmen's feet! (4)

(205)

Gauri V

O! My Immortal Lord!
Why in Your fearless company
Need I be afraid at all? (1)

In one house You are full of conceit;
In the other You are humble and meek.
In one house You are all-in-all;
In another You are much too small.
In one house You give learned discourse;
In another You are stupid and coarse.
In one house You are ever grabbing;
In another You would touch nothing (2)

I am a mere marionette of wood,
The player would understand what He should.
I act the way the Operator directs,
Dress in the garments which He selects. (3)

He has created all the abodes,
Himself He looks after us.
I live in the house where He keeps me,
How can the poor creature refuse?
He who has brought about would know,
The One who has created the entire Show. (4)

Says Nanak, He is the Limitless Master,
Knowing the value of what He is after. (5)

(206)

Gauri V

It is rare that one has his thirst assuaged.
He collects millions and billions,
Yet his mind is not caged.
He asks for more and more. (1)

He has charming wives of every type,
Yet he haunts the neighbour's door,
With no sense of fair and foul on his part. (2)

In the various ties of Maya caught,
Lauding not the Treasure of Virtue
His mind is in evil fraught. (3)

He whom He blesses dies in life.
In the company of the Holy, he is free from
* strife.*
Says Nanak, he is accepted at the door in a
* trice.* (4)

(213)

Gauri Majh V

Who could be the solver of this riddle for me?
The One who is the Creator, perhaps, He could
    be.
Whatever he did was in ignorance;
He did not pray to God nor engage in
    penance.
His mind wandering in ten directions,
Then why indict him with sanctions? (1)

He considered himself master of his will,
His actions and his wealth.
That as long as he was there
With him they would abide.
Lost in such illusions and love,
His feet with a tether tied. (2)

How could he do anything good
When he existed not indeed?
When the Immaculate and the Formless One
Did Whatever He pleased. (3)

He who has created this world,
Plays His own flute.
Says Nanak, the Creator Himself is the Doer,
The True Guru has solved this riddle. (4)

(216)

Gauri V, Majh

Your Name relieves suffering,
Suffering is relieved by Your Name.

I repeat it day and night.
The True Guru has given the insight.
The heart where dwells the Supreme One,
Charming is that frame.
The Yama dare not come near it
The tongue that repeats the Name. (1)

Neither did I serve nor contemplate on God.
I had faith in You, my Measureless,
    Inaccessible Lord. (2)

My Master took kindly,
My sorrows and torments ended,
Neither any ill affected me,
When the True Preceptor defended. (3)

The Guru is God, the Guru is kind.
The Guru is the True Creator.
With the Guru's grace I gained everything;
Nanak is ever sacrifice to the Master. (4)

(218)

Gauri V

He who kills it is a hero indeed.
He who kills it is never in need.
He who kills it is verily great.
Of sickness he is never afraid.
He who kills duality and forsakes.
To Raja Yogi he certainly makes. (1)

He who kills it is afraid not.
He who kills it is in the Name engrossed.

He who kills it his thirst is slaked.
He is freed at the Heaven's Gate. (2)

He who kills it is born wealthy.
He who kills it is honour-worthy.
He who kills it is rid of carnal passion.
He who kills it attains salvation. (3)

He who kills it his visit is auspicious.
He who kills it is ever prosperous.
He who kills it is the one with stake.
He who kills it is always awake. (4)

He who kills it is liberated in life.
He who kills it is free from strife.
He who kills it gains the lore superfine.
He who kills it attains the poise Divine. (5)

He who kills it not, has to wait,
Do a million good deeds, undergo austerities
  and contemplate.
He who kills it not, is condemned to
  transmigration.
He is not free from Yama's persecution. (6)

Without killing it you gain not verity.
Without killing it you wash not impurity.
If you kill it not, everything is unclean.
If you kill it not, evanescent is the entire scene.
  (7)

He to whom the gracious God is kind,
He is liberated, success he finds.

He whose duality is killed by his Lord,
Says Nanak, he would gain awareness of God. (8)

(237, 238)

Gauri V

I remember the Guru every moment of the day;
The Guru is my breath, my mainstay.
I live as I glimpse my Guru.
I drink the wash of His feet true. (1)

I bathe in the dust of my Guru's feet
And thereby shed my old conceit. (2)

I play the refreshing fan for my Guru,
He who protected me from the fiery fury. (3)

For my Guru's household I carry water;
The Guru who gave me the wisdom of
   hereafter. (4)

I would work for my Guru the daily grindstone,
He who befriends for me my foes forsworn (5)

The Guru to me this life gave,
He who bought me as His slave. (6)

Himself He infused His love in me;
I should adore Him ever, this is my plea. (7)

Gone are my aches, worries, fears and woes,
As the accomplished Guru of Nanak
   bestows. (8)

(239–40)

Gauri V

Dear my Lord! Bless me with Your Name.
Without the Name is accursed the love-game.
Without the Name who eats and dresses,
He's like a cur who licks the unclean
   molasses. (1)

Without the Name all the activity
Is vain, like dressing up a dead body. (2)

He who forgets the Name and enjoys
   delectation
Has no peace in dream, suffers affliction. (3)

Forsaking the Name who labours hard,
His doings are false, his manners fraud. (4)

He who does not on the Name dwell,
Despite what he does must go to hell. (5)

He who does not contemplate on the Name,
Like the thief the Yama must one day frame. (6)

All the show and all the ceremonial
Without the Name is false and trivial. (7)

Only he can God's Name remember,
Says Nanak, whom His grace administers. (8)

(240)

Gauri V

Give me your ear, my friend!
Let us try and cajole the Lord.
Shedding conceit, with the Name as dope,
Entangle Him uttering the charm of the Word.
Once He weds, dear friend, He must keep
  company,
This is the way of the Master of Destiny.
Relieves the fear of age, death and hell.
Says Nanak, He has cleansed ever so many. (1)

Give me your ear, my friend!
Following the council wise, let us turn a page.
In a spell of poise, sans distraction, we sing
  the Master's praise.
Afflictions would disappear and fears would
  vanish.
We shall attain what we cherish.
He is Supreme, the Perfect Lord.
In the company of Nanak we remember God. (2)

How I wish and long my friend!
If He were to grant my prayer,
Thirsting for the touch of His feet
And yearning for His gracious stare,
I look for Him here and there.
Finding Him in the company of Godmen,
The One who is for His prowess known.
Says Nanak, it is the lucky ones
Who meet the Supreme Lord of all Perfection. (3)

My friend! I live with my dear Master.
I have endeared myself to God.
Give me your ear, my friend;
I welcome my sleep when I go and meet my
  Lord.
My fears vanished, I am at peace with my
  Love,
Illumined in a poise, the lotus has blossomed.
I have found my Lord Omniscient
Nanak's union is consummated. (4)

(249)

Acrostic V

There is but One God,
Who is realised through the grace of the True
  Guru.

Slok

Charm infinite, high caste, shrewd, learned and
  wealthy,
If she adores not God, says Nanak, she is like
  a dead body.

(253)

Shedding conceit, I am at peace.
My body and mind are sans disease.
Now Nanak can clearly gaze,
The one who is worthy of praise.

(260)

On merit I am at a loss,
I go wrong every moment.
The pardon-giver must pardon me
And cruise Nanak across.

(261)

With the pen in your hand, my Inaccessible
  Lord,
My destiny You wrote on my forehead, true.
Unique in charm, You are involved in all.
My tongue cannot praise;
I long for a glimpse to die for You.

(261)

Sukhmani
(The Pearl of Peace)

Raag Gaudi
by
The Fifth Guru

There is but One God.
He is realised through the grace of the True Guru.

Canto I
Prologue

I salute the Primordial God.
I salute the One preceding Him.
I salute the True Guru.
I salute the Enlightened Lord.

Octavo

Remember Him and thus be blessed,
Shedding anguish and agony.
Remember the One who prevails over all,
Whose Name is on countless lips.
Verified Vedas, the Puranas and Smrities
Are created by His Name Divine.

Whoever is blessed with an iota of it.
He is beyond all praise.
Those who long for His glimpse,
Nanak is sustained by a look at their face. (1)

Sukhmani is the Nectar of the Master's Name.
It brings peace to the devotee.
Meditating on God one is not born again.
Meditating on God drives away the dread of
  death.
Meditating on God frees from the ravages of
  time.
Meditating on God annihilates the enemy.
Meditating on God no harm can ever come.
Meditating on God one remains God-conscious
  day and night.
Meditating on God one fears none.
Meditating on God no malady maligns.
Meditating on God in concert with the Holy
Bestows blessings on Nanak in God-imbued
  company. (2)

Meditating on God proffers physical, mental and
  spiritual treasures.
Meditating on God gives knowledge, devotion
  and essence of wisdom.
Meditating on God is austerities, oblation and
  adoration.
Meditating on God dissolves the canker of
  duality.
Meditating on God is taking Holy dips at
  places of pilgrimage.

Meditating on God begets honour in Heaven.
Meditating on God one does nothing but good.
Meditating on God the success is complete.
He alone can meditate who is blessed by Him.
Nanak would verily sit at his feet. (3)

Meditating on God is the supreme service.
Meditating on God many a seeker is elevated.
Meditating on God arrests the longing for wealth.
Meditating on God makes aware of the
   happenings around.
Meditating on God delivers from the fear of
   death.
Meditating on God fulfils all desires.
Meditating on God frees the mind of filth;
And the Nectar of His Name comes to reside
   in it.
With the Name of God on the devotee's
   tongue,
Nanak is the slave of such a one. (4)

Those who meditate on God are well-to-do.
Those who meditate on God are respected.
Those who meditate on God are accepted.
Those who meditate on God are considered
   superior.
Those who meditate on God look to no one.
Those who meditate on God rule over the rest.
Those who meditate on God live in peace.
Those who meditate on God are in constant
   bliss.

*Those whom the Benevolent Lord bestows His
 remembrance,
Nanak seeks the dust of their feet. (5)*

*Those who meditate on God do good to others.
Those who meditate on God I am sacrifice
 unto them.
Those who meditate on God are pleasent to
 behold.
Those who meditate on God are peace-loving.
Those who meditate on God master their self.
Those who meditate on God tread the path of
 righteousness.
Those who meditate on God enjoy many
 pleasures.
Those who meditate on God live close to Him.
With the grace of the men of God, remember
 Him night and day.
Says Nanak, it is the fortunate who remember
 His Name and pray.   (6)*

*Meditating on God brings success in ventures.
Meditating on God one suffers no regrets.
Meditating on God is singing His praises.
Meditating on God is dissolving in His steady
 vision.
Meditating on God one's seat remains stable.
Meditating on God the lotus blossoms.
Meditating on God is hearing the unstruck
 melody.
There is no end to the joy of meditating on
 God.*

He alone meditates on Him whom He blesses.
Nanak sits at his feet, who the True One
    professes. (7)

It was God's meditation that revealed Godmen.
It was God's meditation that brought forth the
    Vedas.
It was God's meditation that produced miracle
    men, celibates and philanthropists.
It was God's meditation that made the lowly
    known in the four quarters.
It was God's meditation that led to the creation
    of the Universe.
One must meditate on the One who is cause of
    all causes.
All the forms of life we owe to God's
    nomination.
God Himself lives in His Divination.
To whom He blesses, says Nanak,
The Guru-conscious attains God through
    meditation. (8)

Canto II
Prologue

O, the Reliever of the pain of the poor and
    Helper of the helpless!
I come to Your refuge with the blessings of
    Nanak (the selfless).

Octavo

Where mother and father, son, friend and
  brother cannot help,
The Name of God comes to your rescue.
Where the dreadful emissaries of death
  demolish,
The Name of God stands by you.
Where you have untold hardships to bear,
The Name of God rescues you there.
While many other measures may fail to win,
The Name of God will wash your sins.
Remember the Name in the manner of the
  Guru,
And gain the manifold blessings of the True. (1)

Unhappy is the sole monarch of the world,
Remembering the Name he feels felicitous.
The millions and billions bind you down,
Remembering the Name one gets relieved.
The joys galore don't quench your thirst,
To allay it you need the Name of God.
The path that you've to tread alone,
In the company of the Name you feel at home.
Such a Name you remember ever,
The Guru-conscious this way finds His favour. (2)

Where millions and billions do not bail you
  out,
Remembering the Name will set you free.
Where many a crisis threaten your ruin,
Remembering the Name relieves you in a
  moment.

Many a time you are born and die,
Remembering the Name you attain salvation.
Smitten with conceit that cannot be washed,
Remembering the Name kills countless sins.
With a spirited heart remember the Name
That can be attained in the company of
   saints. (3)

In the journey whose length cannot be
   measured,
The Name of God becomes your treasure.
The path that is dark and dusty,
The Name of God makes it lofty.
The voyage where no one knows you,
The Name of God is your boon-companion.
Where the Sun blazes and it is scorching hot,
The Name of God provides you shade.
Where you are thirsty with parched lips,
There Nanak's God gives Nectar dips. (4)

The Name of God is the mainstay of saints.
The men of God are at peace with themselves.
The Name of God is succour of the slave.
The Name of God absolves countless men.
The saints sing His praises day and night.
The ascetics earn the specific by meditation.
For a man of God the Name is liberator.
It is a gift of God to the born mortal.
Those whose self is immersed in the Name,
Says Nanak, they are gifted, Godly and sane. (5)

The Name of God is both the design and
delivery.
The Name of God satisfies the body and sways
the soul.
The Name of God is man's charm and
splendour.
Meditating on the Name one never falters.
The Name of God is every one's glory.
The Name begets praise from all and sundry.
The Name of God is both indulgence and
renunciation.
Meditating on the Name,' one is never at a
loss.
Nanak is devoted to the Name of God,
He keeps meditating ever on the Lord. (6)

The Name of God is man's goods and treasure.
God Himself bestows the Name on the mortal.
The Name of God is man's support and
succour.
Excepting God's glory one knows not anything.
The devotee is merged in the image of God.
In the retreat of the void he is attuned with
the Divine.
He who meditates on God all the while,
God's devotee gets known, he cannot hide.
Meditation on God begets emancipation for man.
Says Nanak, many have along the devotee
swam. (7)

The Name of God is the Parjat* tree.
The Name of God is the Kamdhenu** cow.
To talk of God is the best dialogue.
Listening to the Name banishes sorrow and
*   pain.*
The man of God adorns Him in his heart,
And with His favour he sheds gloom.
Only the fortunate acquire the company of
*   saints.*
In the company of the saints they recite His
*   Name,*
There is nothing to compare with the Name of
*   God.*
Says Nanak, not many are devoted to the Lord.
*   (8)*

Canto III
Prologue

Many a Shastra and Smrities I have searched
*   and seen.*
Nothing compares with the Name; the Name
*   remains Supreme.*

Octavo

Remembrance and asceticism, gnosis and
*   meditation,*
The eight Shastras, the Smrities and their
*   commentaries,*

---

*   A mythical wish-fulfilling tree
** A mythical wish-fulfilling cow

Yoga exercises and formalities of Karma and
*   Dharma,*
Abandoning everything and going to the jungle,
Making many an effort,
Giving alms, indulging in charity, offering gems
*   to the sacrificial fire,*
Also bits of the conceited body,
Undertaking fasts and varied rituals,
Yet nothing compares with the repetition of the
*   Name,*
Not even once if one remembers the same. (1)

You may live long and move about the nine
*   continents of the earth.*
You may withdraw from the world and become
*   the supreme ascetic.*
You may offer yourself to the sacrificial fire,
Give in charity your gold, fine bred horses and
*   land.*
You may undertake Niyoli Karma* and other
*   Yoga practices;*
Adopt the Jain Dharma path and such other
*   disciplines.*
You may make the mince-meat of your body
And yet you will not be rid of your ego.
There is nothing like God's Name for the
*   initiated.*
Says Nanak, the devotee meditates on the Name
*   and is emancipated.* (2)

---

*   A yogic exercise for cleansing the bowels
    for better concentration.

Dedicating oneself to the Deity, one may be rid
  of avarice,
Yet ego and conceit in the mind remain intact.
One may take one's bath day and night,
Yet filth of the mind persists in the body.
One may try and discipline oneself in varied
  ways,
Yet one cannot shake off evil thoughts.
What if one washes the body with water daily,
How can the clay structure be cleaned?
The glory of God's Name is great indeed,
It has the worst sinners redeemed. (3)

Trying to be clever, the fear of death
  overwhelms.
Far too many efforts satisfy not the self.
Changing garbs curbs not the fire inside.
No smuggling in Heaven even with a million
  strides.
Escape in the skies may not release from the
  bondage.
Your lust will land you in the net of sin.
Whatever else you do, it will lead you to
  death.
Without God's praise nothing will help.
Meditating on the Name relieves all strain.
What Nanak says is simple and plain. (4)

He who longs for the four gifts,
He must serve the saints in shifts.
He who wants to be relieved of worry,
He must sing the praises of Hari.

He who looks for name and fame,
Must forsake ego in the company of saints.
He who fears being born again,
The men of God he must entertain.
He who hungers for the Master's glimpse,
Guru Nanak is sacrifice unto him. (5)

Among the mortals·he is supreme,
In the company of saints who has shed conceit.
He who considers himself small,
He indeed is the biggest of all.
He who is the dust of others' feet,
Meditates on God in his heart's retreat.
He who entertains no malice in his mind,
His Lord in the world at large he finds.
He who treats alike pleasure and pain,
Says Nanak, evil and good are no longer his
bane. (6)

Your Name is the fortune of the poor.
Your Name is the home of the homeless.
Your Name is the pride of the humble.
You are the One who sustains all souls.
You are the Doer of all the deeds.
You are in the know of every mind.
You alone know Your extent and limit.
You are Yourself involved in You.
Yourself You adore Yourself.
Says Nanak, none else knows about You. (7)

Of all the faiths the best one is
Remembering God and doing good deeds.

Of all the good deeds the best one is
Shedding evil thoughts in the company of
   saints.
Amongst all the initiatives the best one is
Meditating on God ever and ever.
The most sacred among all the Scriptures is
Listening to God's praises and singing the
   same.
Of all the places most hallowed is
The heart where resounds the Name. (8)

Canto IV
Prologue

O the simpleton of little worth! Remember God.
He Who created you,
Bear Him in your heart
So that He stands by you.

Octavo

Man! Remember the gifts of God.
From what humble origin He lifted you?
He Who created, moulded and adorned you.
He Who nourished you in the mother's womb.
He Who fed you on milk as a child, and
   several dainty dishes.
He Who provided luxurious living in the prime
   of youth,
And near and dear ones, while old
To feed and nurse the invalid in you.
The one without worth will never realise these
   gifts!
Says Nanak, it is Your mercy that can make
   him see it. (1)

With Whose grace you live in comfort
In the happy company of your wife, child,
  brother and friend.
On Whose account you have cold drinks,
Soothing winds and cosy fire.
With Whose grace you have varied pleasures,
A life lavish with luxuries to live in.
Who bestowed you with hands and feet, ears,
  eyes and tongue,
How do you forget Him and take to others?
An unmitigated fool, drowned in delusion;
Says Nanak, only God can redeem you from
  ruin. (2)

He Who is your Saviour in the beginning and
  end,
Him you do not adore, you wretch!
*Serving whom you attain Nine Treasures,**
The stupid! you would not remember Him?
The Master who is ever present before you,
How blind of you to imagine, He is far away!
In whose service you gain glory in heaven
The senseless fool! how can you forget Him,
He is a defaulter always;
Says Nanak, the Saviour must protect him. (3)

Forgetting the gems, you look for shells.
Ignoring the truth, you choose untruth.
What is ephemeral you treat as permanent.
He who is close, you think He is far away.

---

*   Nine treasures of Kubera, god of wealth

You bother about what you will abandon here.
You care not for Him who will abide by you.
You remove the sandal wood paste and wash
  your face,
And fond of dirt you roll in filth.
The sinner has fallen into the pool of delusion
Says Nanak, God can save him in His
  profusion. (4)

Born a human being, you behave like a beast.
You mislead people day and night.
Inside the camouflage there is filth of Maya;
It cannot be hidden, you may try as much.
In appearance you are learned, a Yogi and
  living a clean life,
Within you lives the dog of greed.
With the fire inside, you are reduced to ashes.
With the stone around your neck, how do you
  cross the abysmal ocean?
They in whose heart the Lord resides,
Says Nanak, they are lucky, they live in a
  stride. (5)

The blind cannot find the way from what he
  hears.
Give him a hand and he will arrive at the
  goal.
How can the deaf solve a riddle?
If you talk of night, he will imagine it is
  morning.
How can the dumb sing a song?
Even if he tries, his voice will fail.

How can a cripple stroll on a mountain?
He can hardly scale it even.
My Beloved Creator! I beseech You please,
Nanak the humble, Your mercy may release! (6)

He Who is your constant companion, you
  remember Him not.
You love the one who is your foe.
Living in the house built of sand,
You indulge in play and pleasure of Maya,
Considering it's going to last forever.
The stupid, you remember not the death;
Ill will, strife, lust, anger and attachment,
Falsehood, vice, greed and fraud,
You have lived many a life in their company.
Says Nanak, only God can save you in His
  mercy. (7)

You are the Master, I pray to You.
My soul and body are dedicated to You.
You are my mother and father, I am Your child.
With Your blessings my joy goes wild.
No one knows Your extent, O God!
You are the Super Supreme, my Lord.
The world is Yours, You wield the wand.
Those who are Yours, obey Your command.
You alone know Your nature true.
Nanak the slave is sacrifice unto You. (8)

Canto V
Prologue

Ignoring the bountiful, you seek new brief.
Says Nanak, nothing will avail,
Without the Name you'll come to grief.

Octavo

You run after ten gifts;
If one is withheld, you lose your wits.
Denying even one, if He were to take back ten,
Tell me the simpleton! what would you do then?
The Master Who is beyond reproach,
With all respect we should approach.
Those who delight in His Name,
Their heart remains in excellent frame.
Those whom He makes do His will,
All their needs will Nanak fulfil. (1)

The Divine banker proffers gifts,
One eats and drinks and makes merry.
Were He to take back a part of them,
The ignoramus feels sorry.
This is how one loses faith
And then he is trusted no more.
One should give to Him what belongs to God
And happily accept the command of the Lord.
He would then bless you four-fold,
Says Nanak, the Master is gracious, generous
  and more. (2)

Many a pleasure of Maya
Eventually must come to an end.
You have cultivated the shade of a tree,
It must recede for you to regret.
Whatever you see must die,
You are attached to it in utter delusion.
He who gives himself to a wayfarer,
He gets very little as his share.
O man! Attachment to the Name alone gives
  felicity.
Says Nanak, He brings about the union in His
  mercy. (3)

Myth is the man, his riches, family and the rest.
Myth is the ego, attachment and other
  delusions.
Myth is the authority, youth, wealth and
  prosperity.
Myth is man's lust and his dreadful anger.
Myth is chariots, elephants, horses and robes.
Myth is the seeming charm of life.
Myth is perfidy, perjury and pride.
Myth is taking airs uncalled for.
What will live is the meditation with men of
  God.
Nanak contemplates on the Name sitting at the
  feet of the Lord. (4)

The ears that hear slander are false.
The hands that misappropriate other's fare are
  false.

The eyes that covet the charm of another's
wife are false.
The tongue that relishes dainty dishes (other
than simple food) is false.
The feet that travel for misdeeds are false.
The greedy heart that is ever craving is false.
The body that does not do anyone good is false.
The odour that provokes evil thoughts is false.
All those who refuse to understand this are
false.
Says Nanak, the one who remembers God, he
alone succeeds over all. (5)

Wasted is the life of the Godless,
How can he be truthful without truth?
Wasted is the body without the Name,
And the mouth giving foul smell.
Without the Name day and night go waste,
Like the crop dying without rain.
Adoring not God everything else goes waste
Like wealth in the custody of a skinflint.
Blessed are those who have enshrined the
Name in their heart,
Nanak is sacrifice unto them all. (6)

You do something and hold forth something
else.
Sans devotion in the heart, you pay mere lip
service.
God the Omniscient is aware of everything.
The outward display pleases Him not.
You preach to others, what you practise not.

You come and go, you are born, you die.
He in whose heart is the Fearless enshrined,
The entire world would follow his kind.
Those whom God blesses, they realise Him
indeed.
Nanak would sure propitiate their feet. (7)

I pray to God who is Omniscient.
He who exalts His own creations.
Himself He takes decisions.
To some He appears close while to others at a
distance.
Without trying to be too clever,
He knows what goes on in one's mind.
He whom He blesses, he takes to His kind.
He is here, there and everywhere.
He alone serves Him whom He commends.
Nanak was emancipated remembering Him for a
moment. (8)

Canto VI
Prologue

I come to the refuge of my Lord
With the grace of the Guru.
Pray free me of passion and anger,
Also of greed, attachment and ego.

Octavo

With Whose grace you enjoy half-a-dozen
dainty dishes,
You must bear that Master in mind.

*With Whose grace you enjoy sweet-smelling
  perfumes,*
Remembering Him you attain salvation.
*With Whose grace you live in a comfortable
  abode,*
You must meditate on Him ever and more.
*With Whose grace you enjoy peaceful family
  life,*
You must have Him on your lips all the while.
*With Whose grace you indulge in pleasures of
  every sort,*
*Says Nanak, you must remember the ever
  memorable Lord.* (1)

*With Whose grace you have luxurious-linens to
  wear,*
*How can you forget Him and get attached to
  another?*
*With Whose grace you sleep in a peaceful bed
  of pleasure,*
You must sing His praises day and night.
With Whose grace you are known all over,
You must sing His praises with your tongue.
With Whose grace you protect your Dharma,
You must meditate on Him alone.
*Remembering the Lord you gain glory in
  Heaven,*
*And return to your Eternal Home with honour
  profusion.* (2)

*With Whose grace you have a body healthy
  and glowing,*

You must concentrate on that loving God.
With Whose grace your honour is protected,
You will be happy remembering His Name.
With Whose grace all your lapses are covered,
You must submit to that Great Master.
With Whose grace none with you may vie.
You must remember Him every breath of your
*   life.*
With Whose grace you have this rare form,
Says Nanak, you must meditate on His
*   charm.* (3)

With Whose grace you have ornaments to wear,
Why must you not cherish His memory?
With Whose grace you have horses and
*   elephants to ride,*
You must never forget that Lord.
With Whose grace you have gardens, grounds
*   and riches,*
You must keep Him close to your heart.
With Whose grace you have been moulded
*   grand,*
Remember Him whether you sit or stand.
You should remember the One who is
*   Incomprehensible,*
He will protect you here and hereafter. (4)

With Whose grace you indulge in charity and
*   give alms,*
You must meditate on Him every moment.
With whose grace you are known for your form,
You must remember the Lord in every breath
*   you take.*

With Whose grace you appear so pleasing,
You must keep Him ever in your mind.
With Whose grace you belong to a high caste,
Remember that God day and night.
With Whose grace you are vindicated,
Says Nanak, with the blessings of the Guru you
should sing His praises. (5)

With Whose grace you hear melodious music,
With Whose grace you see enchanting sights,
With Whose grace your speech is nectar-sweet,
With Whose grace you live in comfort and
peace,
With Whose grace your organs function
gracefully.
With Whose grace you live fruitfully.
With Whose grace you attain salvation,
With Whose grace you gain satisfaction,
Abandoning such a Master, why must you seek
someone else?
It is with Guru's grace that Nanak's soul is
blessed. (6)

With Whose grace you are known the world
over,
Don't you ever forget that Lord.
With Whose grace you gain glory,
Oh my stupid self! remember Him ever.
With Whose grace is your purpose achieved,
You must consider Him ever present.
With Whose grace you realise the Truth,
Listen, my dear, you must cling to Him.

With Whose grace we all are saved,
Nanak remembers and to Him he prayed. (7)

He remembers Him whom He initiates.
He sings His praises whom He motivates.
It is with God's grace that one is enlightened.
It is with His grace that the lotus blossoms.
It's in His pleasure He comes to abide by you.
With His grace understanding improves.
Everything worthwhile is born with His
blessings.
One can achieve nothing on one's own.
Whatever You assign to me, O Lord, I do,
Says Nanak, I could hardly do a thing without
You. (8)

Canto VII
Prologue

He is Unapproachable, Immeasurable,
He who remembers Him, only he is saved.
Listen, O friend! what Nanak has to tell;
It is an enchanting discourse of the Holy men.

Octavo

In the fellowship of the Holy, one feels
elevated.
In the fellowship of the Holy, the filth is lost.
In the fellowship of the Holy, vanity vanishes.
In the fellowship of the Holy, blossoms the
gnosis.

*In the fellowship of the Holy, God appears to
be close.*
*In the fellowship of the Holy, the problems are
resolved.*
*In the fellowship of the Holy, one gains the
jewel of the Name.*
*In the fellowship of the Holy, one comes to rely
on the Divine.*
*Says Nanak, who can acclaim the virtues of
the Holy?*
*The glory of the Holy is reflected in the Lord
Sublime.* (1)

*In the fellowship of the Holy, one encounters
the Invisible.*
In the fellowship of the Holy, one prospers ever.
*In the fellowship of the Holy, one can control
the five senses.*
*In the fellowship of the Holy, one enjoys sips
of Nectar.*
*In the fellowship of the Holy, one feels like the
dust of everyone's feet.*
*In the fellowship of the Holy, one's dialogues
become sweet.*
*In the fellowship of the Holy, one wavers no
more.*
*In the fellowship of the Holy, one comes to
gain stability.*
*In the fellowship of the Holy, one is above
temptation and greed.*

*Says Nanak, in the fellowship of the Holy, God
is mighty pleased.* (2)

*In the fellowship of the Holy, the foes become
friends.
In the fellowship of the Holy, one is free from
evil.
In the fellowship of the Holy, one bears malice
to none.
In the fellowship of the Holy, there is no
faltering from the path.
In the fellowship of the Holy, no one remains
no good.
In the fellowship of the Holy, one meets the
Lord God.
In the fellowship of the Holy, one suffers no
mishap.
In the fellowship of the Holy, one is free of
ego.
The greatness of the Holy is known to God.
Says Nanak, the Holy man is attuned to the
Lord.* (3)

*In the fellowship of the Holy, one remains
disciplined.
In the fellowship of the Holy, one is at peace
with oneself.
In the fellowship of the Holy, one perceives the
Unperceivable.
In the fellowship of the Holy, one bears the
unbearable.*

In the fellowship of the Holy, one attains the
Supreme status.
In the fellowship of the Holy, one arrives at
His Palace.
In the fellowship of the Holy, one finds Dharma
all over.
In the fellowship of the Holy, it is only God
one lives with.
In the fellowship of the Holy, one is blessed
with the treasure of the Name.
Nanak, indeed, is sacrifice to the Holy men. (4)

In the fellowship of the Holy, one emancipates
the entire tribe;
Also friends, relations and their people.
In the fellowship of the Holy, one receives
Divine Treasure,
And in return one bestows it on others.
In the fellowship of the Holy, the emissary of
Death is at one's command.
In the fellowship of the Holy, the angels of
Heaven sing one's songs.
In the fellowship of the Holy, one is rid of the
curse of sins.
In the fellowship of the Holy, one hails the
Nectar of the Name.
In the fellowship of the Holy, one feels at home
everywhere.
Says Nanak, in the fellowship of the Holy, life
is a pleasure. (5)

In the fellowship of the Holy, there is no long wait.
A glimpse and you are glorified.
In the fellowship of the Holy, the darkness is dispelled.
In the fellowship of the Holy, Hell is distanced.
In the fellowship of the Holy, one is blessed here and hereafter.
In the fellowship of the Holy, the wayward unites with the Lord.
Whatever one longs for the devotee must get.
The fellowship of the Holy is never in vain.
The Lord Himself lives in the Holy man's heart.
The audience of the Holy is a blessed lot. (6)

In the fellowship of the Holy, one hears God's Name.
In the fellowship of the Holy, one sings His praise.
In the fellowship of the Holy, one forgets not the Master.
In the fellowship of the Holy, one is saved in the end.
In the fellowship of the Holy, one endears oneself to God.
In the fellowship of the Holy, one finds Him in every soul.
In the fellowship of the Holy, one learns to be obedient.
In the fellowship of the Holy, one is hale and hearty.

*In the fellowship of the Holy, all the ailments
depart.*
*Says Nanak, it is fortunate meeting a man of
God.* (7)

*Of the glory of Holy men even the Vedas are
not aware.*
They recount as much as is already there.
*The glory of the Holy men is unlike anything
on earth.*
*The glory of the Holy men can be witnessed
all over.*
The glory of the Holy men has no limit.
The glory of the Holy men begs description.
The glory of the Holy men is higher than high.
*The glory of the Holy men is greater than
great.*
*The glory of the Holy men is its own measuring
yard.*
*Says Nanak, there is no difference between a
Holy man and God.* (8)

Canto VIII
Prologue

Truthful of thought and truthful of word,
He does not see other than the Lord anywhere.
*Says Nanak, these are the features of the God-
aware.*

Octavo

The God-realised is ever untainted,
Like the lotus remaining dry in water.

The God-realised is sans any malice,
Like the sun providing warmth all over.
The God-realised discriminates not,
Like the air sustaining the high and low.
The God-realised remains unruffled,
Like earth ploughed here and propitiated there.
This is the virtue of the God-realised,
Like air he must retain its poise. (1)

The God-realised is cleaner than the clean,
The way water would catch not waste.
The God-realised has his mind illumined,
Like the sky flushed over earth.
Foes and friends are alike for the God-realised.
The God-realised is never conceited.
The God-realised is higher than the high.
The God-realised is lowest of the low.
They alone are God-realised
Who have God Himself as the Guide. (2)

The God-realised is utterly humble.
He alone enjoys the Spiritual bliss.
The God-realised is kind to all.
The God-realised does no harm.
The God-realised is even-handed.
The God-realised rains Nectar sweet.
The God-realised is beyond any bondage.
The God-realised is clean in his dealings.
The God-realised is on the gnosis sustained.
Says Nanak, lost in God the God-realised
    remains. (3)

The God-realised has faith alone in God.
The God-realised knows not death.
The God-realised is humility incarnate.
The God-realised is the fountain of fellow-
feeling.
The God-realised knows no constraint.
The God-realised is ever disciplined.
The God-realised does nothing but good.
The God-realised is ever successful.
The God-realised serves big and small.
Says Nanak, the God-realised is adored by
all. (4)

The God-realised is always the same.
The God-realised lives in the company of the
Lord.
The God-realised has the Name as his tome.
The God-realised has the Name as his home.
The God-realised is ever alert.
The God-realised forsakes conceit.
The God-realised has the Master enshrined in
his heart.
The home of the God-realised is ever in bliss.
The God-realised lives in peace and calm.
Says Nanak, the God-realised never comes to
harm. (5)

The God-realised is aware of the ways of God.
The God-realised is attached to the Lord.
The God-realised is anxiety free.
The God-realised has a crystal-clear mind.
He is God-realised whom He favours.

The God-realised is praised a lot.
The fortunate alone have a glimpse of the
*   God-realised.*
I am sacrifice many a time to the God-realised.
A God like Shiva is in God-realised's quest.
Says Nanak, the God-realised is divinity at
*   best.* (6)

The God-realised is beyond any assessment.
The God-realised has everyone in his ambit.
None knows the mystery of the God-realised.
The God-realised is ever adored.
What the God-realised says cannot be
*   interpreted.*
The God-realised is the Master of us all.
None can measure greatness of the God-
*   realised.*
Only the God-realised knows the secret of the
*   God-realised.*
The God-realised is beyond any limit.
Nanak must to the God-realised submit. (7)

The God-realised is the Creator of the
*   Universe.*
The God-realised lives forever, never dies.
The God-realised creates, acquires salvation, and
*   guides.*
The God-realised is man-perfect ordained by
*   God.*
The God-realised is the refuge of the
*   refugeless.*
The God-realised takes everyone in his fold.

The Universe is in the image of the God-
  realised.
The God-realised is the Formless incarnate.
The God-realised alone can the God-realised
  recall,
Says Nanak, the God-realised is the Provider of
  all. (8)

Canto IX
Prologue

He who has enshrined the Name in his heart,
He who sees the Lord in every part,
He who remembers the Master every breath,
Says Nanak, such a recluse saves the rest.

Octavo

(He who) would not let a lie touch his tongue,
Craves to have a glimpse of the Formless;
(He who) would not cast a glance on another's
  wife,
Remains in the company of saints to serve the
  godly;
(He who) does not hear anyone's slander,
Considers himself poorer than the poor;
(He who) forsakes evil with the grace of the
  Guru,
Gets rid of temptations of the mind;
He whose flesh is free from the five maladies;
Says Nanak, such a recluse is rare to find. (1)

He is Vaishnav with whom the Lord is pleased;
Keeps himself clear of the delusion of Maya;

Acts without consideration of the reward;
Such a Vaishnav can claim True Dharma.
Never looks for fruits for his endeavour;
Remains engrossed in meditation and adoration;
Remembers God in his mind and body;
Takes kindly to everyone around;
Himself remembers and creates motivation;
Says Nanak, such a Vaishnav attains
  salvation. (2)

He is true adherent of Bhakti cult who
  advocates love of God;
Steers clear of the evil-minded;
Discards the duality of mind;
Adores the Lord in everything around;
Removes the filth of sin in the company of the
  Holy;
Such a protagonist of Bhakti cult is pure of
  mind.
He serves God day and night;
Sacrifices his body and soul at the altar of the
  Lord;
Enshrines the Master in his heart;
Says Nanak, such a follower attains God. (3)

He is Pundit who disciplines his mind;
Cultivates the Name of God in it;
And drinks the essence of the Name.
The world is sustained by words of such a
  Pundit.
He has the legend of God inscribed in his
  heart.

Such a Pundit is never to be born again.
Understanding essentials of the Vedas, Puranas
   and Smrities,
He sees the tangible in the abstract.
He whose Sermon is common for the four
   strands,
Nanak salutes such a Pundit with folded
   hands. (4)

The seed of Name is sown in every heart.
Anyone of the four castes can remember the
   Lord.
He who remembers, is emancipated.
Few forsooth gain the Godman's company.
With His grace when He comes to be enshrined
   in the heart,
The Cattle and the spirits, the stupid, and the
   stones are ferried across.
The Name is the remedy for every malady,
And adoration of His Name, is fountain of
   felicity.
Dharma is not to be had, try as we may.
Says Nanak, He alone finds whom He shows
   the way. (5)

He whose heart is the abode of God,
He is the true servant of the Lord.
He who has vision of the Divine,
He becomes slave of the entire clime.
He who sees God close to him ever,
He is admitted to the council of Heaven.

If He is gracious, He blesses His slave;
As if enlightened, so does he behave.
Dwelling with all he remains aloof;
Nanak is the slave, this is the proof. (6)

Ordained by God who surrenders in strife,
He has gained emancipation in life.
The pleasure and pain are alike for him.
He is always happy, never in sorrow.
Gold to him is as good as pelf.
Nectar and poison make no difference.
Honour and dishonour both are similar.
The king and pauper to him are familiar.
Whatever happens he hails it as a prize.
Says Nanak, such a one gains emancipation in
   life. (7)

Every place belongs to God;
Where He abides He acquires a new Name.
He is the Creator and produces all those who
   create.
What happens is as God pleases.
He is spread like the waves of a vast ocean.
No one can imagine the ways of the Lord.
We see Him as we are enlightened by Him.
He is the Overlord, ever-living Creator.
He is ever and ever kind.

Blessed is Nanak bearing Him in his mind. (8)

Canto X
Prologue

Many a seeker sings His praises,
There is no end to His piety.
Says Nanak, it is God who has created the
    Universe
With all its manifold variety.

Octavo

(There are) millions of worshippers;
Millions who perform their duty;
Millions who have taken abode at the places of
    pilgrimage;
Millions who roam in jungles as recluses;
Millions listen to the recitation of the Vedas;
Millions who undergo asceticism;
Millions who meditate on Him;
Millions of poets who adore Him in verse;
Millions who remember Him ever with a new
    Name;
(And yet) says Nanak they fail to ascertain. (1)

(There are) millions who are egocentric;
Millions are blind and ignorant;
Millions are wooden-hearted misers;
Millions are stone-hearted spiritualists;
Millions who misappropriate others' riches;
Millions who talk ill of others;
Millions who are busy amassing wealth;
Millions fond of travelling abroad;

All of them do as they are commissioned to do;
Says Nanak, the Creator alone knows the secret
of His crew. (2)

(There are) millions of seers, celibates and Yogis;
Millions of monarchs living in luxury;
He has created millions of birds and snakes;
Brought about many a mountain and trees;
Elements like air, water and fire;
There are ever so many countries, continents
and planets;
The Sun, Moon and the galaxy of stars;
Deities, demons and crowned kings like Indra;
The entire creation is organised His way,
Says Nanak, He liberates us as and when He
may. (3)

(There are) millions who are wise, wanton and
wicked;
Those who have studied the Vedas, Puranas,
Smrities and their commentaries;
Millions of gems and jewels in the bed of the
ocean;
Millions of variegated living beings;
Millions of those who live long;
Millions of hillocks and mountains of gold;
Millions of Jakhas,* Kinras* and Pisachas;*
Millions of evil spirits, swines and tigers;
He is so close yet so far, far away;
Says Nanak, contained in Himself, He has a
vast sway. (4)

---

* Mythical spirits, good and evil

*(There are) millions who dwell in the
    underworld;
Millions who live in Hell and Heaven;
Millions are born and die;
Millions who reincarnate again and again;
Millions who sit and eat;
Millions who tire themselves working;
Millions are made millionaires;
Millions who keep worrying for wealth;
They behave the way He commands;
Says Nanak, everything remains in God's
    hands. (5)*

*(There are) millions who have withdrawn from
    the world;
They are engrossed in the Lord's Name.
Millions are in quest of God,
Looking for Him in the recesses of their heart.
Millions who long to have a glimpse of God;
And the Eternal Lord comes to meet them all.
Millions who yearn for the company of
    Godmen,
Those who are imbued with His Name.
He whom He comes to favour,
Says Nanak, he is blessed ever and again. (6)*

*(There are) millions of species and the regions
    where they live;
Millions of spheres and their planets;
Millions are born;*

In millions of ways they are propagated;
And the process is repeated many a time.
The Lord God, however, remains the same.
Millions and millions of diverse varieties
Emanate from God and merge in Him.
Nobody knows the limit of the Lord,
He is born from Himself, Guru Nanak's God. (7)

(There are) millions of devotees of God
Who have their minds enlightened.
Many who seek the essence of Truth;
They see none other than Him everywhere.
Millions enjoy the Nectar of His Name.
Immortalised they live forever and ever.
Millions who hail the Lord's Name.
In Spiritual ecstasy they are lost in peace and
  poise.
Those who are dear to Him,
Says Nanak, the Lord makes them swim. (8)

Canto XI
Prologue

God is the Master-Doer,
There is no other hand.
Nanak is sacrifice unto Him
Whom he finds in sea and land.

Octavo

He is the Doer and He alone can do,
What He proposes must accrue.

The Creator creates in no time,
None can know His limit sublime.
With His command He sustains the
  unsustainable.
Withdraws with His command and then makes
  available.
Deeds good or bad are as He pleases,
His pleasure is reflected in moods and their
  phases.
He does Himself and admires His glory,
Says Nanak, He Himself figures in every
  story. (1)

If it pleases God, man is emancipated.
If it pleases God, the stones are floated.
If it pleases God, one lives without air.
If it pleases God, one sings His fare.
If it pleases God, the sinners He retrieves,
He does as best as He conceives.
He is the Master here and hereafter.
The Omniscient plays in smiles and laughter.
What He pleases, He makes us do;
Guru Nanak has none other in view. (2)

Say, what can the man do?
What He likes He would have us pursue.
Left to him, he would grab everything;
The slave must do what pleases the king.
Not knowing, one gets on the evil way;
If he knew, he won't go astray.
Misled he would go all over;
In a moment savour both sweet and sour.

In His mercy if He grants His love,
His Name, says Nanak, would descend from
  above. (3)

In a moment he elevates the lowest of the low,
God is gracious to the poor.
He who has nothing to commend him,
In an instant he would be in everyone's know.
Those to whom He takes kindly,
He cares not for their good or bad deeds.
All the bodies and souls belong to Him.
The Perfect Lord shines in everything.
Himself He has written the entire story,
Nanak enjoys witnessing His glory. (4)

One can do nothing on one's own;
The Lord God is the sole architect.
The helpless man is at His command;
Whatever He ordains that must happen.
At times he is optimist, while at others a
  pessimist.
At times he is happy while at others unhappy.
At times he indulges in slander and scandal,
Soaring high at others, then descending in
  wrangles.
At times the master of all the Divine lore,
But the encounter with God, says Nanak, is on
  God's own score. (5)

At times he dances varieties of dances,
While at others he remains asleep day and
  night.

At times he is in a savage rage,
While at others he is dust of others' feet.
At times he styles himself as a Raja,
While at others he is a beggar of little means.
At times he is talked ill of,
While at others he is praised all over.
One must tread the path God lays,
It is the Truth, that the Guru-enlightened
    Nanak says. (6)

At times he is a Pundit giving discourses,
While at others he is a mum ascetic lost in
    meditation.
At times he bathes at places of pilgrimage,
While at others he is a practised Sidh with
    Divine lore on his lips.
At times he is an elephant, at others a moth,
He wanders from one life to another.
Like a mask-player he plays many roles.
He does the way God writes the score.
Invariably it happens the way He wants,
None other, says Nanak, can give it a slant. (7)

At times he sits in the company of Godmen.
There is no getting away from it.
His soul then gets enlightened,
He is settled there for good.
His mind and body get absorbed in the Name,
He lives constantly in the company of the   Lord.
The way water gets mixed with water;
The way light gets absorbed in light;
His wanderings come to an end, he finds piety.
Nanak is a hundred times sacrifice to such a
    deity. (8)

Canto XII
Prologue

Happy is the humble
Who lives in self-effacement.
Many an egoist has fallen
Because he is arrogant.

Octavo

He who suffers from the kingly pride,
The dog will be lowered into Hell.
He who is proud of his physical charm,
He would end up as a worm of filth.
He who prides in multiple affairs,
He is born and dies to be born again and
*   again.*
He who throws his weight for his wealth and
*   land,*
He is stupid, blind, slow to understand.
He who has learnt to be humble in his grace,
Says Nanak, he is liberated here and goes with
*   a liberated face.* (1)

Do not be proud of your wealth;
It is like straw, nothing will accompany you.
He who banks on his many-flanked forces,
In a moment the whole lot will be lost.
He who thinks himself mightiest of all,
Could be reduced to ashes at a moment's call.
He whose ego would brook none other,
At the Dharamraja's ridicule he would shudder.

With God's grace who sheds the conceit,
Says Nanak, he is welcome to Heaven's
   retreat. (2)

A million deeds done in conceit
Are an effort wasted like dust of the feet.
Undergoing penance in ascetic pride,
From Heaven to Hell perforce one slides.
He does a lot but softens not his heart,
How can he go to the Kingdom of God?
He who calls himself good,
Goodness has not near him stood.
He whose mind is inclined to be humble,
Says Nanak, a man of repute, he never
   stumbles. (3)

As long as he thinks, he is on his own,
Peace of mind he would not have known.
As long as he thinks I am the doer,
He keeps on visiting the womb of his mother.
As long as he makes foes and friends,
His mind to poise would never lend.
As long as he is given to worldly pleasure,
He must expose himself to Dharamraja's ire.
It is God's grace that breaks the chains;
Says Nanak, it is Guru's grace that one ceases
   to be vain. (4)

Having earned a thousand, one longs for a
   million;
He's never satisfied even if he had a trillion.

He engages in many an evil deed,
He lives and dies without his craving appeased.
Without contentment you have no esteem,
All your efforts are like an empty dream.
The ecstasy of the Name brings absolute peace,
It is the fortunate few who have this treat.
He does and Himself creates those who do,
Says Nanak, Him alone you should woo. (5)

The Creator of doers is Himself a Doer;
The mean mortal has little in his power.
The man becomes what God makes of him.
The Lord God has the power to trim.
Whatever He does, it is by His design.
He keeps His distance and yet He is close.
He sees, assimilates and discriminates.
He is one and yet He is many.
He does not die or disappear, nor does He go
*   and come.*
Says Nanak, He the Immortal prevails
*   everywhere in sum.* (6)

Himself He preaches, follows Himself.
He creates the creation with the help of the
*   created.*
Himself He spreads Himself out.
Everything is His, He is the Doer;
There is nothing apart from Him.
He is here, there, everywhere.
He conceives and play-acts Himself;
Many a wondrous parts He plays.

*He is in everyone's mind and everyone is in His
    mind.
Says Nanak, there is no evaluating His design.* (7)

*The Master is truthful,
Only a few with Guru's grace realise it.
Whatever He does is right,
Not many in a million are aware of it.
He is the image of virtue,
Charm incarnate and Peerless.
Sweet indeed are His words;
Heard by ears and absorbed by the heart.
Unalloyed, He is Holy indeed,
Nanak repeats His Name sweet.* (8)

Canto XIII
Prologue

*He who submits to a saint's sanctuary,
He is no more in chains.
Slandering a saint, says Nanak,
Is dying and being born again and again.*

Octavo

*Slandering a saint hastens one's end.
Slandering a saint, one is chased by death.
Slandering a saint one loses all peace.
Slandering a saint is courting Hell.
Slandering a saint the mind gets dirtied.
Slandering a saint is soiling one's reputation.
He who slanders a saint is sheltered nowhere.
Wherever he goes the place gets polluted.*

If the saint in his mercy is kindly and fair,
The slanderer, says Nanak, swims across the
   river. (1)

Slandering a saint gives a sorry face.
Slandering a saint is croaking like a crow.
Slandering a saint is living the life of a
   serpent.
Slandering a saint is a reptile incarnate.
Slandering a saint one's hunger is never
   satisfied.
Slandering a saint one loses one's shine.
Slandering a saint one is lowest of the low.
Slandering a saint one finds shelter nowhere.
Says Nanak, if the saint so desires, even the
   slanderer is spared. (2)

The slanderer of a saint is a hard-core
   extremist.
The slanderer of a saint gathers no moss.
The slanderer of a saint is an arch criminal.
The slanderer of a saint is punished by God.
The slanderer of a saint loses his Raj.
The slanderer of a saint is unhappy and
   helpless.
The slanderer of a saint suffers from several
   ailments.
The slanderer of a saint feels like a cast-off.
The slanderer of a saint is ever frustrated.
Says Nanak, if the saint so desires, the
   slanderer too is liberated. (3)

The slanderer of a saint remains unholy.
The slanderer of a saint is no one's friend.
The slanderer of a saint is penalised by God.
The slanderer of a saint is forsaken by all.
The slanderer of a saint is a confirmed conceit.
The slanderer of a saint is given to
*   unbecoming deeds.*
The slanderer of a saint is born and dies.
Slander a saint and there is no end to
*   suffering.*
The slanderer of a saint abides nowhere.
Says Nanak, if the saint so desires, the
*   slanderer too is reared. (4)*

The slanderer of a saint is abandoned in
*   midstream.*
The slanderer of a saint achieves no objective.
The slanderer of a saint wanders in wilderness.
The slanderer of a saint is lost in a desert.
The slanderer of a saint is hollow from within.
Like the corpse of the dead, slanderer is
*   without breath.*
The slanderer of a saint has no roots.
The slanderer of a saint reaps what he sows.
No one is the ally of the slanderer.
Says Nanak, if the saint so desires, he can
*   reclaim the wanderer. (5)*

The slanderer of a saint laments and wails,
Like a fish thrown out by the gale.
The slanderer of a saint is never quenched,
Like the fire's hunger for the fuel unspent.

The slanderer of a saint is left all alone,
Like the spurious sesame in the harvest zone.
The slanderer of a saint is without any
  Dharma.
The slanderer of a saint is a liar by Karma.
The slanderer acts the way he was designed.
Says Nanak, that must happen what is in God's
  mind. (6)

The slanderer of a saint has a disfigured face.
The slanderer of a saint is punished in His
  state.
The slanderer of a saint is left ever in lurch.
Neither dead nor alive, it is a peculiar perch.
The slanderer of a saint has never his wish
  fulfilled.
The slanderer of a saint is unhappy, gets
  killed.
The slanderer of a saint knows no satisfaction.
He is moulded by the God of All Perfection.
No one can alter the predetermined font.
Says Nanak, it always happens the way He
  wants. (7)

All hearts belong to Him, He is the Creator.
Our obeisance is due to Him.
One must adore God day and night.
He should be remembered every breath of life.
Whatever happens is ordained by Him.
It happens the way He dictates.
It is His play; He acts in it.

None other may comment on it.
He whom He blesses He bestows His Name.
Says Nanak, He alone can fortune claim. (8)

Canto XIV
Prologue

Give up being too clever,
Before God the Great you should bow.
With faith in Him alone,
Says Nanak, your ills, anxieties and fears
  would go.

Octavo

It is in vain relying on man;
The giver is only the Great Bhagwan.
He Whose gifts appease our wants;
And no more longings come to haunt.
He Who kills and can also save,
Man has only for Him to crave.
Carrying out whose command brings you peace;
Keep Him ever in your heart's crease.
Remember, remember, remember Ram,
Says Nanak, remembering Ram, you'll never
  come to harm. (1)

Adore the Formless in your heart;
A truthful journey you must embark.
With untainted tongue the Amrit you sip;
With joyous peace it must equip.
With eyes view the Master's splendour;
Accept the Holy, the rest you surrender.
Tread the path shown by Gobind,

Remembering every moment will rid you of sins.
Serve God with hands and with ears hear His
word.
Says Nanak, this way you will be exonerated in
His Court. (2)

He is blessed in the world
Who sings His praises.
Those who contemplate on His Name
They are really rich.
They are the elite who remember Him by word
and keep Him in mind.
They are known to be ever in peace.
They observe God alone all around.
They are privy to the secrets of this and that
world.
He who is attuned to His Name and State.
Says Nanak, He has known the Immaculate. (3)

With Guru's grace one gets to understand
oneself,
And all his wishes are fulfilled.
He who repeats His Name in the company of
Godmen,
He is rid of all ailments.
He who sings His praises day and night,
He attains emancipation, living even a family
life.
He who has faith in God,
His bonds of mortality snap.
He who hungers for his Ram,
Says Nanak, he never comes to harm. (4)

He who is attuned to God,
He is sound-hearted, he never wavers.
He who is blessed by God,
Why should he fear anyone else?
He can be perceived as He is,
He figures in every activity.
I have comprehended Him after assiduous
*   search.*
With God's grace I have learnt the secret.
Wherever I see, I find Him at the root.
Says Nanak, He is abstract; He is concrete. (5)

No one is born nor anyone dies.
It is all the play of the Lord.
Coming and going, visible and invisible,
The entire world obeys His command.
He Himself exists in everything around;
Varied are His ways to create, establish and
*   destroy.*
Imperishable, He never decays.
He organises the Universe His own way.
Unseen, Inscrutable, a Master of fame,
Says Nanak, if He so desires, one remembers
*   His Name.* (6)

He who has understood God, he is the man of
*   glory.*
He can save the entire world with his message.
He who serves God can uplift many.
He who serves God can relieve suffering.
Himself the Merciful brings about the Union.
Repeating the Name one is blessed.

Only he takes to His service
The fortunate one to whom He is kind.
Meditating on the Name leads to eternal rest.
Says Nanak, among his fellows, he is the
  best. (7)

Whatever he does it is marked by divinity.
He lives in the company of the Lord.
He lets things happen as they come,
Considering that it is the Creator who does it
  all.
Whatever God does, he accepts with pleasure.
He finds God reflected everywhere.
He merges in the One out of whom He was
  born.
Only such a one is entitled to the joy Eternal.
Himself He brings glory to Himself (in man).
Says Nanak, God and His devotee belong to
  the same clan. (8)

Canto XV
Prologue

God is all-powerful.
He is aware of my problems;
Remembering Him I am relieved.
Nanak is sacrifice unto Him.

Octavo

The broken ties are mended by God.
Himself He takes care of His flock.

He who has tender solicitude for all;
There is none beyond His pale.
One must ever bear Him in mind,
Omnipresent and self-reliant.
On one's own, one achieves not a bit,
Howsoever one may yearn for it.
None else is, therefore, of avail to you,
Says Nanak, His Name alone will stand by
*   you.* (1)

He who is comely need not be proud,
It is God's light that reflects in every face.
Why must the rich be vain
When all the wealth is Lord's gift?
He who claims to be a great hero,
Without God's grace what could he achieve?
He who prides in being a philanthropist,
God the Giver considers him stupid.
With Guru's grace he who sheds the curse
*   of vanity,*
Says Nanak, only he is healthy in all the
*   humanity.* (2)

The way a pillar supports the structure,
So does the Guru's word enliven a heart.
The way a stone loaded in a boat can go
*   across,*
The man dedicated to the Guru can be
*   emancipated.*
The way the light dispels darkness,
A glimpse of the Guru kindles the mind.
The way one finds the path in wilderness,

The company of the Holy illumines the soul.
Look for the foot-dust of such a saint,
Says Nanak, God will allay your plaints. (3)

Man! why must you foolishly howl?
You reap what you sowed earlier.
It is God who grants weal and woe.
Forgetting the rest, remember Him alone.
Whatever He does, accept it with pleasure.
Don't you get misled ever.
What is it that you brought with you?
Like a greedy moth you are given to gaiety.
Repeat the Name of Rama in your mind,
Says Nanak, this is the way to glory for your
     kind. (4)

The merchandise that you came to purchase,
It is Rama's Name you acquire at the saints'.
Shedding your pride, swap your soul
And weigh the Name in your heart's scale.
Load your goods and go with the godly,
Give up all the trappings of evil.
Everyone must hail you then.
With a beaming face you enter Heaven.
Few are those who pay this price.
Nanak is unto them sacrifice. (5)

Wash the feet of the Holy and drink it.
Dedicate your soul to the Holy.
Bathe in the foot-dust of the Holy.
Offer your life for sacrifice to the Holy.
Sing God's praises in the company of the Holy.

It is great luck serving the Holy.
The Holy can save one from many a calamity.
You adore God and have sips of Amrit.
He who seeks the Holy and comes to his beat,
Says Nanak, all the comforts are his treat. (6)

God gives life to the dead.
He provides succour to the hungry.
Man looks for many a treasure,
But he gets what is ordained by Him.
Everything belongs to Him; He is the Doer,
There is nothing outside His pale.
Man! repeat His Name day and night,
It is indeed the best of occupations.
He whom He grants His Name in His grace,
Says Nanak, he is the one with a Sublime
  face. (7)

He who has the awareness of the Guru,
He is the one who remembers God.
He hears the Name of the Lord all over,
He who has God in his heart.
What he does is truthful on a truthful rung,
He has truth in his heart and truth on his
  tongue.
His vision is truthful; he embodies truth.
Truth is his wherewithal, he propagates truth.
He who has found God forsooth,
Says Nanak, he is indeed absorbed in truth. (8)

Canto XVI
Prologue

Without a figure, features and form
God is beyond the Three Norms. *
He makes Himself manifest
To him whom He has blessed.

Octavo

Keeping the Eternal God in mind,
Forget the attachment of any kind.
There is nothing beyond my Lord.
He is reflected in every heart.
He sees all; He knows all;
Deep and discerning, profound above all.
He is Parbrahm, Parmeshawar and Gobind,
Kind and merciful, quick to rescind.
I long for a seat at His feet,
Says Nanak, this is for which my heart beats. (1)

He fulfils wishes and provides' solace,
Whatever He desires must take place.
His glance, and things are made and unmade,
No one knows the secret of His trade.
Joy incarnate, He is the fountain of pleasure,
His home is said to be a virtual treasure.
He is a Raja among Rajas and Yogi among
  Yogis,
Ascetic among ascetics, also a man of family.

---

* Three Norms are: Enlightenment, Serenity
and Spontaneous devotion.

The devotees remember Him and enjoy it much,
Says Nanak, none has been able to know Him
as such. (2)

He whose wonders have no limit;
All the angels who have tried, submit.
How can the son know the father's birth?
He has tied with a thread the entire earth.
Only those devotees meditate on Him,
Who are granted good sense, knowledge and
vision.
The world of senses becomes whose woe,
They are born and die, come and go.
High and low are the Lord's stations,
Man could know only what He sanctions. (3)

He has several figures and several forms;
Many a guise and yet He retains His norm.
Many are His manners, He is spread far,
The Immortal God is Ikoankar.
Quick He plays His wondrous parts
And yet He is perfect in every art.
In many a way He mounts the sets
And Himself sits to watch the effects.
His are the hearts, His are the places,
His Name alone Guru Nanak traces. (4)

All the living beings live by His Name.
The planets and Universe are in His frame.
The Name supports the Smrities, Vedas and
Puranas,
And all those who listen and go into Dhyana.

The Name supports the netherworld and the
  sky.
The Name supports the low and the high.
The Name supports the cities and the houses.
The Name supports those who listen to discourses.
He whom He bestows the Name in grace,
Says Nanak, he attains the Fourth Stage. (5)

Truth is the form and the devotee's station.
His identity is truth that merits mention.
True are his words and true his deeds;
The true one must in life succeed.
Truthful is what he does, what he creates is
  true,
When the roots are true, true must be the tree.
Transparent, the truthful action is clean,
It is acceptable to those whom He redeems.
The Divine Name of God is comfort true,
Nanak attained his faith from his Guru. (6)

It is truth what the Holy imparts.
They are truthful who have the Lord in their
  hearts.
When one understands the essence of truth,
Remembering the Name the emancipation is
  smooth.
He is truthful, what he accomplishes is truth,
Himself he understands his own worth.
He who has fashioned it, He alone can make it
  function;
None else can know it with cogitation.

The created understands not the extent of the
   Creator;
Nanak makes do with what is willed by the
   Maker. (7)

The seeker is lost in the ecstatic wonder;
He who understands it, enjoys with abandon.
He who lives in the company of the Lord,
He obtains what he wants with the Guru's Word.
He is benevolent, reliever of pain,
In whose company one salvation gains.
He is blessed who waits on Him,
In His company one concentrates on Him.
The devotee sings the praises of the Lord,
With the grace of the Guru, Nanak gets the
   reward. (8)

Canto XVII
Prologue

He was here in the beginning
And before the beginning.
He is here today,
He will be here hereafter.

Octavo

Sacred are His feet and truthful the one who
   touches them.
Sacred is His worship and truthful the
   worshipper.
Sacred is His vision and truthful the one who
   views it.

Sacred is His Name and truthful the one who
  repeats it.
He is truthful Himself and He supports truth.
He is virtue incarnate and imparts virtue to
  others.
His word is sacred and truthful is the one who
  utters it.
Sacred are His perceptions and truthful the one
  who imbibes them.
He who is enlightened, everything is truthful
  for him.
Says Nanak, God alone is true and trim. (1)

He who has realised God as the image of
  truth,
He accepts Him as the Creator forsooth.
He who has faith in God at his heart,
The essence of truth he alone has got.
He becomes fearless when liberated from fear,
And merges back into the source that bears.
It is like something dissolving into another,
No more different one from the other.
The knowledgeable man would know and claim,
God and Nanak are the same. (2)

The devotee of the Lord is a man obedient.
The devotee of the Lord is ever subservient.
The devotee of the Lord is understanding.
The devotee of the Lord has a noble bearing.
The devotee of the Lord has the Master as his
  companion.

The devotee of the Lord has the Name for
  communion.
The Lord God looks after the devotee.
The Invisible Master protects the devotee.
He is the devotee whom the Lord maketh.
Says Nanak, the devotee remembers Him every
  breath. (3)

He vindicates His devotee.
He bears till the end with His devotee.
He brings glory to His devotee.
He makes His devotee meditate on Him.
He protects His devotee's honour.
None dare find fault with his manner.
None can ever compare with the devotee.
The devotee of God is highest among the high.
He whom God engages out of favour,
Says Nanak, he is known the world over. (4)

He reflects His ingenuity in a tiny ant,
And destroys a million strong force if He
  wants.
If He would not have you die
He would keep you high and dry.
The man takes many a measure;
Nothing leads him anywhere.
None else can kill or save;
He is the Saviour of the entire enclave.
What for are you wavering in your heart?
Says Nanak, remember the Inscrutable,
  Wondrous Lord. (5)

Remember the Lord time and again,
Sipping Amrit edifies your mind, muscle and
*   vein.*
The devotee who attains the jewel of the
*   Name,*
No more does he care for anything vain.
The Name is wealth, the Name is health, the
*   Name is love,*
The Name is living in peace with the Lord
*   above.*
Those who are fed with the essence of the
*   Name,*
Body and soul they are merged in the same.
Remember the Name sitting, standing and even
*   sleeping,*
Says Nanak, this should be man's treasured
*   keeping.* (6)

Day and night adore the Lord,
This is the gift bestowed by God.
Meditate on Him with longing soul,
Merging with God remains your goal.
He who abides by the Lord's command,
He has past and future in his hands.
Who can adore such a Lord?
I say it all with utter regard.
He who remembers God all the while,
He indeed is His perfect child. (7)

Solicit His refuge, my heart!
Offering the body and soul on your part.
He who has realised his Master,
He has all others to look after.

Coming to His refuge brings peace,
A glimpse and the sins are washed with ease.
Forget looking around in vain,
Take to His service for any gain.
So that you do not have to come and go,
Says Nanak, hold His feet and solemnly bow. (8)

Canto XVIII
Prologue

He is the True Guru who has realised the True
  Lord.
The devotee earns salvation in His company,
Says Nanak, by constant adoration of God.

Octavo

The True Guru looks after the devotee,
The disciple always finds Him kindly.
The Guru helps the devotee shed the mud of
  misled mind.
Advised by the Guru he meditates on the Lord
  kind.
The True Guru breaks the worldly bonds of the
  devotee.
The disciple is retrieved from the evil company.
The True Guru initiates the devotee into the
  creed,
Such a devotee is fortunate indeed.
The True Guru minds the devotee's ups and
  downs.

Says Nanak, the True Guru cherishes the
   devotee as His own. (1)

The devotee who lives with the Guru,
Abides in His mind by His decree.
Who does not take any airs,
Meditates on God for ever.
He who is entirely sold to Him
Such a devotee suffers no problem.
Serving the Lord he forgets the reward,
And thereby he propitiates God.
He whom He shows His mercy,
Says Nanak, such a devotee subscribes to the
   Deity. (2)

He who is devoted to the Guru unreservedly,
Such a one is privy to his destiny.
The True Guru who is devoted to the Name,
I am sacrifice to him time and again.
The Benevolent One who imparts life,
Absorbed he is in the Master all the while.
Man is in God; God is in man.
There is no doubt He is the One.
He is not attained by a hundred clever ways,
Says Nanak, with such a Guru only good luck
   prevails. (3)

A glimpse is enough to cleanse a man.
A touch of the feet could turn you into a
   swan.
He who sings His praises in the company of
   the Godmen,

He attains access to the Eternal Heaven.
Listening to His words the ears get charmed,
The mind is at rest and the soul is warmed.
Armed with this spell he is a perfect Guru,
His immortalising look makes a saint of you.
His virtues are legion, none may appraise them.
Says Nanak, those He blesses, He would
    eventually raise them. (4)

I have one tongue, Your blessings are many.
You are the One with wisdom uncanny.
I know of no words that can take me to You,
The Transcendental, the Unperceived, my
    Absolute Guru.
Without any want, without any malice, source
    of happiness,
None has ever been able to determine Your
    greatness.
Many a devotee offer their obeisance to You,
Meditate on the lotus feet of the Beau.
I am sacrifice unto my true Guide,
Says Nanak, because of him such a Lord is my
    pride. (5)

Few are those who enjoy meditation on God,
They sip Amrit with salvation as reward.
Such a one never comes to grief,
In whose heart the Lord God lives.
He who sings God's praises all the while,
And inculcates this in his tribe,
He is not embroiled in love of any kind.
God alone he retains in his mind.

As the darkness dissipates by lighting a lamp,
Says Nanak, no more anxiety, attachment and
*   sorrow stay in his camp.* (6)

It turned cool in the sweltering heat.
Sorrow gave place to pleasant treat.
Vanished the fear of life and death,
With the teachings of the Holy adept.
Sans any fear I have become fearless,
With none of the ills my heart is oppressed.
He has blessed to whom I belong,
In the company of the Godmen I sing His
*   songs.*
Attuned to the strains of His melody, my
*   wanderings are tamed,*
Nanak is devoted to hearing the Lord God's
*   Name.* (7)

He is both Absolute and Related.
With His skill of an artist both are mated.
He creates His own wonderments,
Himself He evaluates His establishments.
There is none other than God.
In every being I see my Lord.
Engulfed with His creation in colour and
*   beauty,*
One gets enlightened in the company of the
*   Holy.*
His creation is a reflection of His art sublime,
Nanak is sacrifice to Him many a time. (8)

Canto XIX
Prologue

Besides His Name you carry nothing.
All the rest is sheer puffing.
Acquiring the wealth of the Lord's Name
Says Nanak, is the secret of eternal fame.

Octavo

Reflect on His Name in the company of the
Holy.
Meditate on His Name, His Name is the
remedy.
Give up all other measures, my friend!
Enshrine His lotus feet in your mind.
He is the Master-Doer perfect.
Hold on to His Name, it is certainly worth it.
Collect this wealth and you will be rich.
This is the truth the Holy teach.
Bear in your heart the only trust;
Says Nanak, all your ailments quit you must. (1)

The wealth you go about gathering in the four
quarters,
You gain it in the service of the Master.
The comfort you crave for every day,
Is obtained in the company of men who pray.
The name for which you do good deeds,
Is enjoyed by sitting at His feet.
The malady that no medicine can cure,
With the remedy of the Name it shall disappear.

Of all the cherished gifts the Name is the best,
Says Nanak, remember the Lord and you are
   blessed. (2)

Cultivate your mind with God's Name,
Rather than wandering, stay at home.
He never finds the times any hard,
Who has in his heart the Name of God.
Kaliyug is smouldering, the Name is soothing,
The more you meditate the more it is
   comforting.
You shed the fear, your hopes are met,
With love and devotion your mind is at rest.
You arrive at home and gain salvation.
Says Nanak, this is the way to emancipation.
                                                    (3)

The true one talks of truth as a refrain;
The false one is born, dies, to be born again.
Transmigration is terminated by serving God,
Surrendering oneself and reporting to the Lord.
This way the jewel of life finds the mould,
By repeating His name that sustains the soul.
There is no other way of emancipation,
Even reflecting on the Smrities, Shastras, Vedas
   and their recitation.
Remember God in your heart of hearts,
Says Nanak, this is the way to get what you
   sought. (4)

You carry not with you what you possess,
Why must you then cling to it so much?

Engrossed in son, friends, family and children,
You find not time for His veneration.
Wielding power and indulging in luxury,
How do you expect yourself to be free?
Riding the horses, elephants and chariots,
All this is false without any merit.
He who has given you all this you recognise
   Him not,
Alienated from the Name, Nanak is
   distraught. (5)

The uninitiated! Take the Guru's advice.
Drowned without His Name are many a wise.
My friend! Cultivate the love of God
So that without a smudge you clean your heart.
Keep attuned to His lotus feet
And thereby the evil of ages sweep.
Dwell on His name and help others do so;
He who hears His Name, utters and acts, to
   His home will he go.
The essence of truth is the Name of God,
Says Nanak, sing His praises with a quiet
   heart. (6)

Adoring the Master your sins are washed,
The vicious conceit, vanishes like frost.
Free from care you are rid of strife,
Remembering God every breath of your life.
Give up all your clever manipulations,
In the company of Godmen you find
   redemption.

With the Name as your capital, trade in truth,
You will be peaceful here with your future
  smooth.
The Lord God prevails everywhere,
Says Nanak, only the lucky are aware. (7)

Meditate on One and adore only One;
Think of God alone and none.
Sing His praises who is without end;
To Him your body and soul you lend.
He the Lord God is the only One,
He alone does what is half-done.
It is from One that many are created,
Remembering the One all evils are abated.
Those who have God enshrined in their body
  and mind,
Says Nanak, with the grace of the Guru, they
  do Him find. (8)

Canto XX
Prologue

Having wandered all over
I come to Your presence;
It is Nanak's plea,
Take me in Your service.

Octavo

A supplicant! I come seeking charity
The gift of Your Name, my Celebrity;
I crave for dust of the feet of the Godmen,
The Lord God, do pay heed and listen,
That I sing Your praises in life and death,

That I meditate on You every breath,
That I remain devoted to Your lotus feet,
And remember You as a daily treat.
It is for Your refuge and for Your support I
*   come.*
Nanak begs for the essence of Your Name. (1)

It is utmost comfort if He is kind;
But relish in His Name not many find.
Those who have tasted it, they are satisfied,
They are content, never in a mind-divide.
Intoxicated with love their hearts overflow,
In the company of the Godmen their dedication
*   grows.*
Giving up all else, they seek His protection,
With heart enlightened and mind in meditation.
It is only the fortunate who remember Him.
Says Nanak, absorbed in the Name they are
*   fine and trim.* (2)

The devotee in service is ever satisfied.
He has for a guide the True Guru's advice.
God is gracious to His flock.
Happily grants them whatever they ask.
Their bonds broken, they are liberated
From life and death and doubts created.
Their cravings are met and desires satisfied,
The All-Pervading remains by their side.
He to Whom they belong comes to their rescue.
Says Nanak, longing for His Name they always
*   pursue.* (3)

Why forget Him who will not have you rue?
Why forget Him who appreciates whatever
* you do?*
Why forget Him who has given you everything?
Why forget Him who is the soul of the living?
Why forget Him who protects you from the fire
* (of the womb)?*
It is only the rare one who realises it with the
* Guru's boon.*
Why forget Him who pulls you out of sins?
And ties the long, long broken links?
My Guru Immaculate has shown me the way,
Remembering his Lord, Nanak goes not
* astray.* (4)

I invite you, friends, to play this game.
Forget all else and remember His Name.
Remember Him and be blessed.
Remember yourself and inspire the rest.
In the spell of devotion, you will swim across
* (the ocean of life).*
Without devotion you will be a pile of ashes in
* the strife.*
The Name is Eternal bliss and perennial peace;
The one who is sinking can expect a lease.
All the ills vanish with His courtesy true.
Says Nanak, remember the Name, the Treasure
* of Virtue.* (5)

I have in my heart stirring a soulful love,
My mind and body seem soaring above.
Beholding them with my eyes I feel delighted.

Washing the feet of the Godmen I am elated.
The body and the mind of the Holy are ever in
trance,
Finding their company is a rare chance.
Pray do me only one favour,
With the grace of the Guru I remember You
ever.
No one dare praise You enough,
Says Nanak, the Lord prevails here and
above. (6)

God is forgiving and kind to the have-not.
Protector of the Holy and bountiful a lot.
Helper of the helpless, He is Gobind and
Gopal.
In ever so many ways He helps them all.
He is the Primal, Cause of Causes and the
Creator,
The very breath of those who serve Him as
waiters.
He who meditates on Him, he is relieved.
Love and devotion are His creed.
I am worthless, low and ignorant.
Says Nanak, I come seeking refuge in You,
Bhagwant! (7)

He goes straight to Heaven obtaining
emancipation
Who for a moment takes to His adoration.
He rules over many and enjoys super luxury,
Who cherishes listening to his Master's story.

Dainty dishes, rich clothes and music (are his
    due),
He who every day remembers his Guru.
What he does is virtuous, he has wealth and
    acquires fame.
He has in his heart the Eternal Name.
In the company of the Holy bless me, O Lord!
So that Nanak has the dawn of peace in his
    heart. (8)

Canto XXI
Prologue

He is Absolute and Related,
The Formless sits in a void in an ecstatic state.
He is the Creator Himself,
And Himself makes us meditate.

Octavo

When the creation was not mooted,
Who was then bad and who was good?
When He was in a meditating trance,
For strife and hatred who had the chance?
When He had no feature, no form,
Joy and sorrow then came wherefrom?
When the Supreme Lord was all by Himself,
Who loved whom and who was doubtful?
His is the game and Himself He plays,
There is no other Creator, Guru Nanak says. (1)

When God was the lone lender of money,
Then who was bonded and who was free?

When He was alone without reach and bound,
Why then were Hell and Heaven found?
When the Absolute was in the state of poise,
Shiva and Shakti had but little choice.
When He has infused His own light,
Then who should be unafraid, who be in
*   fright?*
His are the doings and He is the Doer,
Nanak's Master is unknowable, living on an
*   unreached shore. (2)*

When the Eternal was relaxing on His throne,
Who was born, who died and who was death-
*   prone?*
When the Perfect God Himself had created,
Then how could there be the ill-fated?
When the Impersonal and Incomprehensible God
*   was around,*
Then how could Chitragupta ask for accounts?
When the Immaculate Master, Ununderstood and
*   Unrealised hailed,*
Then who could be free and who could be
*   jailed?*
He Himself wondered about Himself there,
Says Nanak, then Himself He created Himself
*   out of nowhere. (3)*

When the Immaculate Lord, the Master of all
*   prevailed,*
Where was the dirt and who did the washing
*   avail?*
In the reign of the Formless, Absolute, and
*   Unattached,*

Who was matchless and who was matched?
When the Creator was the only one there,
Where was the question of being fair and
*   unfair?*
When the contemplated light merges in another
*   light,*
Then who remains dim and who is bright?
He is the Creator who builds and mounts,
Says Nanak, the Doer Himself has little
*   count. (4)*

When He was there with His glory,
How could the parents, friends, sons and
*   brothers form part of the story?*
When He was the reservoir of many-faceted
*   wisdom,*
Where were the teachers of the Vedas and
*   Islamic system?*
When He kept to Himself all the Sermons,
Who ever cared for good and bad omens?
When He Himself was high and Himself low,
Who was the Master and who was to tow?
One is lost wondering about the mystery,
Says Nanak, He Himself should know about the
*   sophistry. (5)*

He who cannot be deceived, who is
*   Invulnerable and Mysterious,*
How could the threat of Maya for Him be
*   serious?*
He would greet Himself (as one of the
*   formalities),*

*There being no practice of the Three Qualities.**
When the Auspicious One was all alone,
Then who was careless and who was care-
  worn?
When Himself He was convinced of the deed,
Then who was to listen and who was to plead?
The Limitless is higher than the high,
Says Nanak, He alone can reach His sky. (6)

When He Himself created the world with His
  skill,
Reflecting Himself in Truth, Energy and Will,
Where was the difference between the good and
  evil?
Whom did Heaven and Hell bedevil?
The network of Maya and its lure,
Conceit, attachment, doubt and fear,
Pain and pleasure, honour and dishonour,
Described differently by different scholars.
It is His drama which He plays and watches
  on His own,
Says Nanak, when He winds the play, He is
  left all alone. (7)

Where there is Deity, there are devotees in the
  image of the Lord.
As He propagates, it is for the glory of the
  ward.
He is the dispenser of both the sides,
Their pride is His own pride.

---

*   Three Qualities are: Enlightenment, Serenity
    and Spontaneous devotion.

He plays many a wondrous roles variously,
And enjoys them all vicariously.
When He is gracious He favours with His Name.
When He is kind, He lets one play His game.
He is beyond calculation, depthless and in a
*   weightless mould,*
Nanak speaks the languages he has been
*   told. (8)*

Canto XXII
Prologue

The Master of all the living beings,
He is reflected in every action.
Says Nanak, He prevails all over,
There is none other for reflection.

Octavo

Himself He observes and Himself listens.
He is One; despite the fact that everywhere
*   He glistens.*
When He pleases He creates the Universe;
When He so desires, He does the reverse.
Nothing happens unless He permits;
With His thread the world He knits.
He whom He enlightens,
Truth becomes his fascination.
Even-minded, understanding the essence of the
*   Verse;*
Says Nanak, He is victorious in the
*   Universe. (1)*

Everything living is in His hands,
By the lowly the kind Master stands.
None can kill him whom He protects,
He is dead whom He forgets.
Giving Him up where can one go
When He is the Master of the Show?
He who holds the key to life,
Home or abroad He is by your side.
Mine of Virtue, Infinite and Endless,
Him alone does Nanak profess. (2)

The Merciful is Omnipresent,
He is kind to every supplicant.
He alone is aware of His ways.
Here and there the Immanent sways.
A variety of living beings He looks after;
Whosoever He has created, remembers the
   Master.
He whom He blesses, him He raises,
The devotee would remember and sing His
   praises.
With faith in his mind he accepts the Lord,
Nanak has realised the Creator Lord. (3)

The man of God who is devoted to the Name,
He has never to come to shame.
The devotee has an opportunity to serve,
Listening to the Lord, in Him He may merge.
There is nothing beyond this stage,
Those who would in meditation engage.
They break their bonds and shed hostility,
Day and night they are at the feet of the
   Deity.

They are peaceful here and happy there,
Says Nanak, the Lord takes them in His
 care. (4)

In the company of the Holy have a good time,
Singing the praises of the Sublime.
Contemplate on the essence of the Name,
A rare opportunity for one to claim.
Adore Him with the ambrosial sweet songs,
This is an opportunity for which you long.
See the Lord by your side all the while;
Shed the darkness and forsake the guile.
Listen to the Gospel and bear it in mind,
Says Nanak, whatever you desire you will
 find. (5)

You will improve both this and life to be,
If you have His Name in your mind's custody.
The Perfect Guru's Gospel, forsooth,
He who cherishes can wrestle with Truth.
He who meditates on Him with devoted mind,
Free from sorrow, pain and fear he will find.
As a trader, deal with Truth alone,
So that in Heaven you are accepted and shown.
Look upon Him as the Master of the Show.
Nanak does not have to come nor has to go. (6)
Giving Him up where can one go?
Remembering the Saviour relieves from woe.
Meditating on the Formless, fears recede,
And man is from bonds of mortality freed.
He who is protected by God suffers no pain,
Meditating on the Name he is free from strain.

Rid of anxieties and shedding conceit,
No one can match His Lofty Reach.
The valiant Guru stands watch over His ward,
Says Nanak, all his problems are solved. (7)

Absolute wisdom and ambrosial glance,
A single glimpse found the world in dance.
Whose lotus feet are beyond applause,
The personal charm in the image of God.
His service is blessed, blessed is the devotee,
A searcher of hearts, the elect of the Deity.
He who cherishes His memory is pleased,
And from the scare of death released.
He is Immortal, lives in the company of the
*   Lord;*
In the fellowship of the Holy, Nanak remembers
*   God.* (8)

Canto XXIII
Prologue

With the kohl of knowledge granted by the
*   Guru,*
My opaqueness of ignorance is gone.
I serve the Holy with the grace of God,
Nanak has entered into a glorious dawn.

Octavo

In the fellowship of the Holy, I have realised
*   God.*
It is sweet indeed the Name of the Lord.
The entire universe is contained in His mind,
And the various colours are therein enshrined.

The ambrosial Name of God is like the Nine
  Treasures,
It is located in the body (as a convenient
  measure).
The unstruck melody heard in the void,
Its wondrous ecstasy cannot be described.
He alone sees whom He grants the light,
Says Nanak, such a one acquires the insight. (1)

The Infinite is both inside and outside,
In every heart the Lord resides.
He is on earth, both underneath and above
And nourishes the world with utmost love.
The Lord God is in the blades of grass, woods
  and mountains,
For all the activity He is the Fountain.
He is contained in air, fire and water,
In ten directions and four quarters.
Devoid of Him there is no space,
Says Nanak, live in peace with the Guru's
  grace. (2)

In the Sun, the Moon and the Stars Him I
  find,
Also in the Vedas, Puranas and Smrities (as
  envisioned by mankind).
Each of them speaks the language of God,
While He remains in poise, the Steady Lord.
He plays the game in various parts,
Measureless in many arts.
He whose light is in every light,
The Master prevails in depth and height.

Those who with the grace of the Guru have
   their doubts shed,
Says Nanak, with faith in God they are blessed.
   (3)

The saint sees God in everything around.
The saint listens to Dharma in his heart's
   sound.
The saint has only auspicious talk to hear,
He has the all-pervading Rama as a peer.
Those who have realised Him, it is their way,
It is nothing but Truth whatever they say.
Whatever happens he accepts forsooth,
Knowing that it is the Creator's Truth.
He is both inside and outside planted,
Just a glimpse and Nanak is enchanted. (4)

He is true, truthful is what He has created.
It is from Him the world has emanated.
If He pleases He spreads Himself far,
If He so desires He contracts into Ikoankar.
His many doings are inscrutable.
To whom He blesses, for him He is ever
   available.
How can He be close and how can He be
   away,
When it is He who has the absolute sway?
He in whom He reveals the secret in essence,
Says Nanak, He realises God's presence. (5)

In all the elements, He is the Doer.
In all the eyes, He is the Viewer.

The entire Universe is God in phases,
Himself He listens His own praises.
The coming and going is for Him a game of
   dolls,
The world remains at His beck and call.
He disguises Himself in many ways;
Whatever is to be said He Himself says
They come and go as He pleases.
Says Nanak, He withdraws them all as His
   interest ceases. (6)

What He does cannot be evil;
Outside Him who could be His equal?
He does nothing but good, good is His kind,
He alone knows what is in His mind.
He is true, truthful is His mission,
And remains enshrined in His creation.
Nobody knows the extent of His self,
Which would be possible had there been
   someone else.
Whatever He does one must subscribe,
With the grace of the Guru, Nanak has
   realised. (7)

He who has known Him is happy.
It is God who reveals Himself to the devotee.
He is rich, of high caste and commands fame,
Immortal in life and a heart full of Lord's
   Name.
Thrice blessed is His arrival;
His arrival assures the world's survival.
The good in arrival of the Man of Destiny
Is that one remembers God in His company.

He is emancipated and the rest He liberates,
Before such a One Nanak prostrates. (8)

Canto XXIV
Prologue

I meditate on the Absolute Lord,
Absolute indeed He is called.
To Nanak has been revealed the Deity,
Whose praises he sings as a devotee.

Octavo

Listening to the Perfect Guru,
You will find God close by you.
Remembering God at every step,
All your anxieties must be swept.
Give up hoping and making complaints,
Ask for the dust of the feet of the saints.
Shed the conceit and make your supplication,
In the company of the Holy, cross the flaming
    ocean,
And fill your coffers with the wealth Divine;
Nanak salutes his Guru Sublime. (1)

Good health and happiness, praise and joy are
    totally
(The reward) for contemplating on God with
    the Holy.
Clearing the Hell you will be raised,
Sipping Amrit and singing His praise.
Remembering God alone in your heart,
Who remains One but plays many parts.

He holds and sustains the world and is kind to
the poor.
He relieves all pains and is the mercy dispenser.
Contemplate on His Name again and again,
Says Nanak, this alone will life sustain. (2)

The valued words uttered by the Holy (as a
rule),
Are priceless gems and invaluable jewels.
He who listens and abides by them is saved;
Himself he swims and for others the path is
paved.
His life is success, his company is a reward,
He who is imbued with the Name of God.
There are strains of celestial slogans of victory,
As one listens one goes into ecstasy.
God is reflected in the forehead of the Holy,
Nanak is saved in such a blessed company. (3)

I come to seek refuge in the One who gives
shelter,
He was indeed kind and allowed me to enter.
The hostilities vanish, I become as humble as
dust,
Remembering the ambrosial Name in the
company of the Just.
The revered Guru has felt pleased,
The devotee's service has this achieved.
All the temptations and misdeeds shed,
The tongue utters the Name it is fed.
The merciful God is gracious and kind,
Nanak with his cargo has arrived. (4)

O my saint friends! let us sing God's praises,
With the singleness of mind and bright faces.
Sukhmani is the state of poise and a hymn of
   God's Name;
He who imbibes it remains in excellent frame.
All that he wishes is fulfilled;
The Lord God to him is revealed.
He acquires the Supreme seat;
 He doesn't have to go and then to retreat.
With the Name as his earning he would repair,
Says Nanak, he who has acquired the profit
   here. (5)

Solace, peace, riches and aesthetic pleasure,
Knowledge, wisdom and odd spiritual measure.
Learning, penance, Yoga and divine repasts,
Highest lore and the choicest baths.
The Four Gifts and blossoming of the lotus,
Remaining amidst all but with a different focus.
Charm, intellect and wit with precision,
Even-mindedness and a single vision.
All these rewards to him are brought,
Says Nanak, he who imbibes the Name in word
   and thought. (6)

If one were to strive to acquire this treasure,
He would be vindicated in every sphere.
It is like God supplicated and the Name
   invocated.
It is like the reading of the Shastras and the
   Vedas recited.

The Name is the essence of all religions,
It resides alone in the hearts of Godmen.
Many a sin are washed in the company of
    liberated.
If the saint is kind, the devotee is emancipated.
God Himself blesses them with opportunity,
Says Nanak, those who seek refuge with the
    Holy. (7)

He who listens with devotion and bears it in
    his heart,
He is the one who remembers God.
He is relieved from the agony of transmigration.
In an instant his soul attains salvation.
A fair name he has and an ambrosial sweet
    tone,
Who has in his heart the Name of God alone.
Gone are his sorrows, maladies, doubts and
    fright;
Known as Godman, what he does is right.
He will be crowned with the highest glory,
Says Nanak, this is the assured gift of
    Sukhmani. (8)

Slok

My sufferings alleviated, doubts removed,
I come to the Lord God's care.
Nanak acheived his heart's desire
Singing the Creator's prayers.

Pauri

*Some sing, others listen and yet others
    contemplate.*
Some take to preaching;
But those who follow, only they arrive at the Gate.
Their sins are washed, they turn clean,
Their filth of ages is no more to be seen.
They remain unsoiled here and hereafter;
Also saved from Maya's disaster.
*They are sophisticated, Vaishnavites, learned and
    wealthy,*
*They are heroes of high caste, who adore the
    Deity.*
*The Kshatriyas, Brahmins, Vaishyas, Shudras
    and even the Chandals,*
*If they adore the Master, Nanak at their feet
    will fall.*

(300)

Slok V

*A beggar, I ask for a dole from my Beloved
    Lord.*
*The ever Bestowing Master, I remember in my
    heart.*
*There is hardly an end to His fathomless
    treasure.*
*Says Nanak, the Word is unique; it is a
    Saviour.*

Slok V

Cherish the Holy Word.
It is the mainstay in life and death.
Contemplating on the One ensures fair face
and good health.

Pauri

Amrit, which brings peace to one and all, is
distributed there,
No one goes the way of death or is annihilated
where.
He who comes to dote on Him, he suffers no
pain.
In the company of Godmen he recites Scriptures
where Amrit seems to rain.
Nanak lives on a glimpse of Him, in a soulful
strain.

(320)

Raga Asa

Asa V

My spouse has parted me from my mother-in-
  law.
Of jealousy are dead sister-in-law and brother-
  in-law.
My older brother-in-law may no more dare;
My wise and worthy spouse takes care.
Listen ye all! I have entered the love game,
The evil wiped out and foes vanquished,
The True Guru has bestowed on me with the
  Name. (1)

As a first step, I shed ego.
Then, ways of the world.
And now alike are, friend and foe.
I merge in the Holy as to the Turiya* stage
  I go. (2)

---

* The mental state of Super-consciousness or
   Samadhi.

In the cave of poise, a seat I have found.
As I am enlightened, the melody sounds.
Ecstatic I delve deep for the Word profound.
Devoted to the spouse, I am blissfully
  bound. (3)

Nanak expounds the Divine lore.
He who listens will arrive at the shore.
He will neither be born nor will he die.
Neither will he come nor will he go.
He will remain merged in the Lord of Yore. (4)

(370)

Asa V

As a first step, just send a letter.
Talking face to face may perhaps be better.
Whatever you do, you must try hard;
But doing all this, think of the Lord.
Rapturous, fearless and full of poise I remain,
My foes and ill-wishers have all been slain. (1)

My True Guru has said it on authority,
The mind and body are God's property.
Whatever I do is ordained by You.
You are my anchor, I'm sustained by You. (2)

But for You, where could I go my Lord?
Nowhere is anyone the like of God.
Your devotee does not care for others.
The non-believer in the jungle wanders.

You are much too great for words, I dare.
Clasping me to your bosom, You take me in
* your care.*
Nanak, the slave craves forYour protection.
He is saved, it is a matter of celebration. (4)

(371–72)

Asa V

As I forget You, everyone pushes me aside.
When I remember You, they turn to my side.
I can visualise no one other than You,
My Truthful, Inaccessible, Unknowable Beau.
Remembering You my Lord ever kind,
The rest of the world I need not mind.
Why must I call anyone good or bad
When everyone belongs to Your squad? (1)

You are my succour, You are my support,
You stretch Your hand, Your devotee you hold.
He to whom you are polite,
None on earth may dare him slight. (2)

What You approve is pleasing and respectful,
Wise and generous, Your Name is delightful. (3)

Pray, my body and mind are Yours, I claim,
But for Your grace, says Nanak, who would
* know my name?* (4)

(383)

Asa V

I go on a pilgrimage, it is only ego I find.
The Pundit, I consult, is with Maya blind.
Dear friend, show me the spot
Where chanting the Name is the daily slot. (1)

I read the Vedas, Shastras, the good and bad
form,
Hell and Heaven, I saw,
I died and was many a time born. (2)

Conceited or worried over family life,
Counting on Karma and daily strife. (3)

It is God's grace which helps one control;
The devotee, says Nanak, is free from Maya's
hold. (4)

Singing His praises in the company of Godmen,
One gains this status if graced by the
Superman.

(385)

Asa V

The low-born for whom no one cares,
If he remembered God, he would be known
everywhere.
Dear Lord! Let me have a glimpse of You.
If You are gracious, who won't be ferried
through? (1)

He whom no one would cultivate,
Before him the whole world would prostrate. (2)

He who is found at the lowest rung,
If the Guru is gracious, his praises are sung. (3)

In the company of the Holy, the slumbering
mind awakes.
Says Nanak, it is only then, one to the Lord
takes. (4)

(386)

Asa V

I was in slumber and prayed not to the Lord.
As the day dawned, I was distraught.
If you long for the Lord, cherish His pleasant
thought.
If you wish to meet Him, then why this sloth? (1)

He offered me Amrit in my hand.
The hand shook and it was strewn on the
sand. (2)

I am lost in the pleasure of worldly love and
conceit.
It is no fault of my Creator Sweet. (3)

In the company of the Holy my doubts are
dissipated.
To the Creator Himself was Nanak related. (4)

(389)

Asa V

Himself He protects the devotee,
And makes him imbibe the Name.
Wherever the devotee has His concern,
He must rush to attend the same.
He assures the devotee that He is close.
Whenever the devotee has a problem,
He instantly arrives thereof to dispose. (1)

I am sacrifice unto the devotee
Whom the Lord God loves.
Even a word from him refreshes.
To Him would Nanak be pleased to serve. (2)

(403)

Asa V Lyric, Score 7

There is but One God,
He is realised through the grace of the True
   Guru.

Slok

Blessed thoughts, contemplation on God
And company of the taintless men of God,
Nanak must forget not the Name for a
   moment,
Do me this favour, my Lord!

Lyric

The night is fragrant and the stars twinkle in
    swarm.
Those who adore God are awake, the beloved
    of Rama.
Those whom God loves are ever awake,
Contemplating on the Name day and night
With their mind set on His lotus feet.
They forget not the Master for a trice.
Shedding conceit, attachment and evil thought
Their suffering and sorrows forsake.
Nanak venerates the Holy who remains ever
    awake. (1)

My bed is done up with lavish care.
I am gladdened to learn of His arrival here.
I met my Master, the pilgrim of peace,
Overflowing with joy and ecstatic release.
As the limb touched the limb, all sorrows fled,
My breath, mind and body were in a moment
    refreshed.
My wish fulfilled I remembered God at the
    auspicious hour.
Nanak prayed and met Sridhar* in a rapturous
    bower. (2)

My friends now ask for the features of my
    spouse,
Delirious with pleasure, I can open not my
    mouth.

---

*   Vishnu–Hari

The virtues of the Creator are deep-rooted,
  endless and disguised,
Even the Vedas cannot their extent realise.
Give the Master loving devotion and His
  praises due accord.
Accomplished and enlightened if you are a
  favourite of the Lord.
Lost in His devotion prayerfully, says Nanak,
You will merge into the Lord. (3)

When I took to singing the Preceptor's praises,
Friends were happy and foes were in blazes.
My comforts multiplied, I was devoted to the
  Name,
The Lord God gracefully deigned to claim.
As I came in His protection, I was ever awake
And met Vishnu of the wild flowers.
It was the advent of the auspicious times,
I attained all the treasures in their own hour.
Prayerfully says Nanak, the devotees hasten to
  the Lord in His bower. (4)

(459)

Raga Gujri

Gujri V

Quartets Score I

There is but One God
Who is realised through the grace of the True
*   Guru.*

Why must you feel anxious
When your Master is at the helm of the
*   affairs?*
He provides for those embedded in rocks
With their feed ever ready there.
Dear my friend! He who cultivates the Holy
*   attains salvation.*
With the Guru's grace he arrives at the top,
Like the dry woods in the course of
*   afforestation.* (1)

The mother, father, friends, son and wife
Nobody comes to one's aid.
The Master provides for everyone.
Why must you be afraid? (2)

She flies hundreds of kos leaving the chicks
   behind.
Who does feed and nourish them?
She remembers them only in her mind. (3)

All the treasures, mystic powers God gives in
   His hand,
Nanak is sacrifice to Him a hundred times.
He cannot fathom His content, nor untangle
   His strand. (4)

                                        (495)

Gujri V, Score 2

There is but One God
Who is realised through the grace of the True
   Guru.

Among the rajas, You are a raja.
Among the landlords, a landlord.
Among the elders, You are the eldest,
And amongst the nobility, the noble You are
   called.

My Father is much too rich and exalted.
How can one praise the Creator?
Seeing Him one is just flabbergasted. (1)

Amongst the happy, You are happy;
Amongst the benevolent, You are benevolent;
And among aesthetes, You are indulgent. (2)

Amongst heroes, You are a hero,
And among the pleasure-loving, the One who
loves pleasure.
Amongst house-holders, You are an ideal family
man,
And among the recluses, ever a recluse. (3)

Amongst the doers, You are a Doer,
And among men of character, You are known
for Your character.
Amongst money-lenders, You are a true money-
lender,
And among traders, You are trader. (4)

Amongst those who hold court, You are the
court.
You are a shelter to those who seek Your
refuge.
Your treasures cannot be counted,
I find them much too huge. (5)

Amongst the celebrated, You are a celebrity,
And among the learned, You are a scholar.
Amongst the men of wisdom, You are wise,
And among those who take ritual baths, You
are the bather. (6)

Among ascetics, You are known for asceticism,
And among performers of rituals, You are a
past-master.
Everyone is under Your charge,
You are the Supreme Commander. (7)

I speak the way You ordain.
I have no other status.
Nanak adores You in the company of the Holy;
Which is dear to You as a practice. (8)

(507–8)

Raga Gujri Var V, Slok

There is but One God
Who is realised through the grace of the True
  Guru.

Remembering the Guru at heart and repeating
  with tongue His Name,
Seeing Him with the eyes and hearing with
  ears the same,
Devoted thus to the True Guru, you fit into the
  Divine frame.
Says Nanak, with His grace whom He bestows
  this favour;
There are only a few who attain this honour. (1)

The Saviour must save; Himself He sustains.
If you fall at His feet, The Lord must retain.
In His mercy He would never let you complain.
In the company of the Holy, He will cruise you
  across the ocean.
The misled, the revilers, the foes are in an
  instant undone.
Nanak has his faith in such a One in his
  heart,
Remembering Whom it gives comfort and all
  sorrows depart. (2)

Pauri

*You are beyond the bonds of tribe, Immaculate
and Inaccessible Lord.*
*Born out of truth, You are true and the
truthful-loving God.*
Nothing appears to be false in Your formation.
You provide for all Your creation.
*Knitting them with a thread, You infuse them
with light.*
*Some are lost in the sea while others go across
the dike.*
*Only he remembers You who is blessed with
Your grace.*
*I am sacrifice to You whose extent I cannot
trace.*

(517–18)

Raga Devgandhari

Devgandhari V, Score 2

There is but One God
Who is realised through the grace of the True
  Guru.

Mother! Let us devote ourselves to the feet of
  the Guru.
If the Lord is gracious, the lotus blossoms.
One adores Him day and night through.
He is inside, outside is He.
He abides in us all.
Pervading every heart and soul
Is my many-splendoured Lord. (1)

Many an ascetic sing Your praises;
Your extent they find not true,
Bestower of comfort and reliever of pain,
Nanak, the slave is sacrifice unto You. (2)

(508)

Devgandhari V

I ask for just one favour Lord!
Kind and Benevolent Master!
Make me a devotee of the men of God.
I should sit at their feet early in the morning
And remain in their presence night and day.
Dedicating my mind and body I serve them
And sing their praises as I may. (1)

Remembering God every breath
And living in the company of the men of God;
The Name be my succour and support,
Nanak yearns for pleasure of the sort. (2)

(533)

Devgandhari V

My love! Sweet are Your words,
Ravishing and beauteous!
You are like everyone and yet You are great.
I ask not for Raj, nor for salvation.
I long for the love of Your lotus feet.
Maybe there are Brahma, Shiva, sages and
    Indra,
I yearn alone for Your sight. (1)

The humble comes at Your door, my Master!
Exhausted he seeks Your light.
Nanak has now met his Enchanter,
His heart is full of delight. (2)

(534)

Raga Wadhans

Wadhans V, Score 1

There is but One God
Who is realised through the grace of the True
Guru.

His Darbar is much too lofty,
Limitless and beyond the comprehension of
mind.
Millions try and make endeavours,
Not clues of the Mansion they find.
what auspicious hour   does one meet the Lord
so kind? (1)

Him on whom a hundred thousand devotees
meditate.
A hundred thousand ascetics in penance
contemplate.
A hundred thousand Yogis practise Yogic feats.
A hundred thousand creatures enjoy treats. (2)

In every heart You live and yet not many
realise Your presence.

*Is there one who has torn this veil of
    ignorance?
If there is one I'll strive for him.
Why, I will even die for him.* (3)

*Having wandered I come to the saints
Who have freed me of my fears and pains.
He asked me over, I had Amrit to drink,
Says Nanak, the Lord is above every other
    thing.* (4)

(562)

Wadhans V

*Blessed is the hour when I have His glimpse.
I am sacrifice unto the Guru's presence.
My Beloved Lord, my being He sustains,
I live only by remembering His Name.* (1)

*True is His Gospel, His word is Amrit.
An image of quiet, His sight is blessed.* (2)

*Eternal are His commands on the throne
    established.
Neither born nor He dies, my Immortal
    Beloved.* (3)

*He is the generous Master, I am His slave.
Nanak's Lord God pervades every place.* (4)

(562)

Raga Wadhans V

. . .My expectation met, my wishes fulfilled.
I am without merit, You are my Master-skilled.
Virtue incarnate, my Lord!
How do I sing Your praises?
You cared not whether I am good or bad;
In a trice you pardoned my sins, their wages.
Blessed with Nine Treasures* and unstruck
*   melodies.*
Nanak found his spouse at home, no more is
*   he worried. . . .*

(577)

---

*   Blessings named after nine different precious
     stones

Raga Sorath

Sorath V

Blessed, I adored the accomplished Guru
And I found my mentor.
My Master was my anchor. (1)

I am sacrifice unto my Divine spouse.
I find peace all around,
There is rejoicing in my house.
The Master who can read one's mind,
Unafraid I sought Him, and the Name helped
me find. (2)

Blessed is His sight in the image of the
Immortal.
He is here today, He will be here hereafter.
With fond love He protects His flock,
Holding it all in His clasp. (3)

Granted great honour, rare esteem and the task
achieved;
Nanak adored the accomplished Guru and was
from ills relieved. (4)

(610)

Sorath V

For those who are happy, everyone appears to
  be happy.
For those who are sick, everyone appears to be
  sick.
It is the Master-Doer who does everything,
It is He who conceives and contrives every
  trick. (1)

Man! He who is rid of doubt and distrust,
For him no one has gone astray;
He sees the Creator at His best.
He who is at peace in the company of saints,
He finds the whole world serene.
He who is afflicted with ego,
Ever he lives and dies in spleen. (2)

He who uses the collyrium of knowledge in his
  eyes,
He gets fully enlightened.
No more does he stumble in ignorance,
Nor is he any more frightened. (3)

Lord! Do grant Nanak's prayer.
He just seeks peace in Thy glory.
Where godmen sing Your praises,
He should set his heart there. (4)

                                          (610)

Sorath V

We are untidy, You are tidy.
We are meritless, You lend us quality.
We are stupid, You are clever and sound;
Aware of whatever happens around. (1)

Lord! we are so low, You are so high.
We are sinners, You annul our sins.
My Immaculate Master of the sky,
You created and gave us life and body.
Good for nothing, without any virtue,
We ask for Your charity. (2)

You are good, we realise it not.
You are ever kind.
You my Creator, are the Bestower of comfort,
Your flock You always tend and mind. (3)

Blessings Incarnate, Eternal Sovereign!
Men and creatures look up to You.
Nanak has only one prayer to make,
Let me follow my True Guru. (4)

(613)

Sorath V

I am the dirt of the feet of the Holy,
They are my guide.
The Holy are my support,
The Holy are my pride. (1)

I am devoted to the Holy,
As determined by destiny.
My mind pledged thereby,
The saints I have cultivated.
I deal with the saints.
Who are given to devotion,
They are my gain. (2)

The Holy bequeathed a boon
And rid me of my doubts.
What can now the Dharmaraja do
When torn is all my account? (3)

I am the recipient of Supreme bliss
Through the goodwill of the Holy
Nanak is devoted to the Divine,
He is dyed in wondrous ecstasy. (4)

(614)

Sorath V

Lost in the blind love of Maya,
You recognise not the One who bestows.
(Forgetting the One) who gave you life and
    body,
To yourself all this, you believe, you owe. (1)

Man! Don't be stupid, He sees it all.
He is aware of whatever you do,
From Him are not hidden big or small.
Engrossed in the delicacies of tongue in greed
That lead to many ills.
Tortured in transmigration
With bonds of ego that kill. (2)

Behind closed doors and veils
You sleep with another's wife,
When Chitragupta asks the account,
Who will save your life? (3)

Kind and compassionate Master, Reliever of ills!
I have none other than You for support.
Pull me through the ocean of the world,
Nanak has come to Your Court. (4)

(616)

Sorath V

The Lord God comes to one's aid,
Telling His tales and singing His songs pays.
One must repeat His Name daily
For utmost bliss and felicity. (1)

Man! you must remember the Truthful.
Enjoy every comfort in the company of the
*   Holy,*
Forgetting not for a moment the Bountiful.
It is like Amrit, the Name of the Lord.
He who repeats it, lives for ever.
Favoured by luck, he is free from fraud. (2)

Devoted to the Guru, I am free from problems
*   and pain.*
Singing praises of the Ever-living, I enjoy His
*   constant strain.* (3)

Blessed is God's discourse.
In the beginning, in the end and in between
He was by Nanak's side, of course. (4)

(616)

Sorath V

The great Guru has been gracious.
All my longings are met.
Singing praises of the Lord
In the Guru's presence I feel at rest. (1)

It is a pleasant image, pleasant and perfect.
Repeating the Name in a quiet poise
The unstruck melody is struck.
I have met my beloved Master.
The temple of my house is blessed.
Nanak has gained the treasure of the Name,
All his prayers are met. (2)

(618)

Sorath V

The Guru-Perfect was kindly inclined.
Everyone turned gracious.
Himself he effected the Union but gave me the
    credit.
It was peace all over and happiness. (1)

With the Guru-Perfect on my side,
The Lord God with me abides.

I see Him inside and outside the house,
Here and there wherever I glance.
Nanak, the lucky, met his Guru,
His Supreme Deity by chance. (2)

(618–19)

Sorath V

Measure not my merit;
Consider Your benevolence;
Save me and extend Your support;
So that ever I partake Your eminence. (1)

With His perennial kindness the True Master
  created.
The Guru-Perfect ended our troubles.
Everyone around was thus liberated.
Infused with life, clothed and fed,
Himself He saved His slave.
Nanak, who is sacrifice to Him and blessed. (2)

(619–20)

Sorath V

The Creator has bestowed peace.
The tribe is at peace.
The Guru-Perfect has brought
The protection of the Truthful I sought. (1)

The Lord Himself helped.
Contentment, truth, peace were acquired in a
  trice;
The mind remained ever blessed.
God's Name worked as a remedy
Which freed me of my malady.
He took kindly
And settled everything smoothly. (2)

The Preceptor came to my rescue
Caring not for my merit or due.
God's Word stood witness
Which accounted for the bliss. (3)

I speak as You ordain.
You, my Virtuous Master, I maintain.
Nanak repeated Your Name as Truth.
You saved the honour of the slave forsooth. (4)

(622–23)

Sorath V

The Creator came and stood by us;
There was no trouble, there was no fuss.
The Guru had the (ritual) bath blessed,
Remembering the Name sins were shed.

Godmen! Ramdas pool is celebrated.
 He who bathes in it his family is saved,
And is himself liberated. (1)

The world sings His praises.
He obtains what he chases.
(The ritual) bath concluded peacefully,
Remembering God gratefully. (2)

He who has a dip in the pool of saints,
He must his Salvation obtain.
He dies not, nor is he born again,
He who has the Name in the grain. (3)

This Spiritual truth only he would mind,
When Almighty the Virtuous is kind.
Coming to Baba Nanak's protection,
Frees one of all worries and affliction. (4)

(623)

Sorath V

Thick dark clouds hover all over,
The lightning flashes with grim scorn.
All alone on my bed and sleepless,
To distant lands has My love gone, (1)

And there is no word from my Don.
Earlier he would go a kos
And pat a missive-private send.
How can I forget my gem of a lover
Every felicity to me he lends?
Going up the house, I watch the way he went,
My eyes full of tears unspent. (2)

My ego has distanced me from him.
Otherwise I hear he is close.
Separated by the (thin) wings of a butterfly
That my mind's eye chose. (3)
When the Master took kindly to me
All sorrows were banished.
Nanak imbibed the All-Pervading Lord
When the wall of ego was demolished.
All my doubts were dissipated,
Whatever I asked for was created,
By my All-Virtuous God. (4)

(624)

Sorath V

The Mender of the broken,
The Liberator from bonds,
The Formless,
The Redeemer from sorrow!
I have no good deeds to my credit,
Nor am I acquainted with Dharma.
I am avaricious,
Playing with the riches; I lend and borrow.
I have come to be known as a devotee of the
    Lord.
Do vindicate my honour, O God! (1)

Dear Lord! You are the pride of the poor.
You make the worthless worthy.
I am sacrifice unto You, my Doer.

The way a child dictated by his nature
Indulges in many a bad deed;
The father reprimands and shouts
And yet forsakes not his seed.
He forgives and forgets the sins
And for future gives the lead. (2)

He can read one's mind,
He knows it all,
Then why ask Him for aught?
He is pleased not with pleas,
If He chooses He grants what is sought.
I have knocked all other doors,
It is only His which I have not. (3)

In His benevolence the kindly Father
Listened to my prayer.
The Guru-Perfect brought about the Union,
My worries gone and seen nowhere.
Treated with remedy of the Name
Nanak found his perennial welfare. (4)

(624–25)

Sorath V

There is but One God
Who is realised through the grace of the
  True Guru.

A dip in the pool of Ramdas,
Washes all the sins of the past.

The Holy bath cleanses,
Which the Guru-Perfect dispenses. (1)

It is peace and plenty everywhere.
Contemplating on the Guru's word
All the dealings are plain and fair.
The malice shed in the company of the men of
    God.
Nanak contemplated on the Word
And met the Primordial Lord. (2)

(625–26)

Sorath V

There is but One God
Who is realised through grace of the True
    Guru.

I read Scriptures, studied the Vedas,
Underwent Yogic discipline of Nival* and
    Bhoingam.*
Yet I could shake off not the five evils,
Caught I was with conceit and egoism. (1)

This is not the way to meet Him, man!
Having tried many a plan
Defeated I come to the Master's door,
Praying for understanding, wisdom and lore.
I took to silence, forsook pots and pans,
Naked in the jungle I roamed,

---

*   Yoga praxis

Also the river banks and temples all over,
Yet the mind-set of duality could not be
forsworn. (2)

I thought and settled at a place of pilgrimage,
Putting my head beneath the sacrificial saw,
Yet malice of the mind could not be shed
However much I tried and longed. (3)

Gold and girls, horses and elephants,
Alms-giving of varied score,
Rich food, dresses and gift of land,
All that takes you not to the Creator's door.
(4)

Worship, adoration, adulation, lying prostrate,
And six disciplines prescribed by Shastras;
Smitten by avarice one is trapped,
None of these takes you to the Master. (5)

You may go through pain and strain,
Yogic and eighty-four postures of ascetics,
You may live long and be born again,
Yet the company of God you may not obtain. (6)

You may rule and have glory and power
Over all and sundry.
Your luxury beds and sandalwood essence
Sure to terrible hell They will carry. (7)

Singing God's praises in company of the Holy
Is great good fortune.

Says Nanak, it is for one
Who has earned this rare boon. (8)

Your devotee is dyed in this colour.
He who helps the needy and relieves the pain
Took kindly to me.
Singing God's praises, I merged in the strain. (9)

(641–42)

Raga Dhanasri

Dhanasri V

You look after us every moment
Our Benevolent Lord, Sustainer and the
  Supreme Master.
We are like little children,
You are the Great Crafter.
How do we sing Your untold praises,
With just one tongue in to count?
Beyond computation, the great Baron,
No one has known Your bounds. (1)

Forgiving our countless sins,
With various ways You guide.
We are ignorant with little understanding;
Do take pity and provide. (2)

We are under Your protection with faith in You.
You are the cherished Spouse.
Save us, Kind Saviour,
We are the menials of Nanak's house. (3)

(674)

Dhanasri V

*He who is all-powerful put His hand on my
    head.*
*A gracious look of the Benevolent and all the
    evils fled.*
*The Lord God took care of the followers of His
    creed.*
*Folded me in His arms and pardoned my
    misdeeds.*
The Lord God gives all that one wants.
*Says Nanak, whatever one utters from the
    mouth,*
Here and hereafter He grants.

(681)

Raga Jaitsri

Jaitsri V

There is but One God
Who is realised through the grace of the True
*   Guru.*

Yearning for His glimpse day and night,
I longed for the communion.
The Guru opened the Gate
And brought about the Union.

Lyric

Listen dear friend! I have a request to make.
I long and thirst for my Beloved's sake.
Give me His tidings
For whose momentary glimpse
I would chop my head and surrender.
My eyes are dyed in His colour,
Not for a moment they cease to wonder.
I long for the Lord like fish for water;
Or a Chatrik in its nest.
When the poor Nanak found his Guru,
All his longings were met. (1)

(703)

Slok

Untold alms and ritual baths
As measures of purification,
Says Nanak, are gained by repeating the Name
And all the sins are washed. (1)

Collect a measure of fuel
Expose it to a little fire.
It is like sheddings all the ills
Remembering the True Sire. (2)

Pauri

Contemplating on the Name
Millions of misdeeds are washed.
Saying the Lord's praises,
One gains whatever one asks.
No more the fear of life and death,
One attains a secure slot.
Only if it is inscribed in the fate,
The Master's presence is sought.
Nanak is sacrifice unto You,
Bless him with a kindly thought. (5)

(706–07)

Raga Todi

Todi V

He is miserable who forgets the Lord.
He who has faith in God fears not the odds.
It is like living in a pit of a snake
The life spent without the Name.
He who rules over the nine planets
Will in the end go empty handed. (1)

He sings songs of the Supreme Adorable,
He to whom You are favourable.
He is happy, blessed is his life,
Nanak is unto him sacrifice. (2)

(711–12)

Todi V

Lord Gracious! Ever You abide with me.
Give me the light and spark
So that I love and adore Thee.
Bless me with dust of the feet of Your slave,
The abject sinner I am cleansed
And sing praises of my Dev. (1)

What You ordain should be acceptable to me.
What You do I should agree.
What you give, I should feel content.
I must not look around and lament. (2)

I should consider my Lord God ever close,
And feel (humble) like the dust of others' feet.
In the hallowed company of Godmen
I should my Preceptor meet. (3)

I am ever your petty menial,
You are my Spouse.
Nanak is like a child, You are my Lord
  forsooth.
Your Name is like the milk in my mouth. (4)

(712–13)

Todi V

Lord! I come for protection to You.
Pray grant me peace and glory of the Name
And free me of my anxiety. (1)

I can think of no other shore.
Disregard my misdeeds galore
Worthless I am, do pull me out.
Ever forgiving and ever gracious,
To everyone You give refuge.
Nanak, the slave, seeks company of the Holy,
Pray, save me this time from the deluge. (2)

(713)

Raga Bairadi

Raga Bairadi V, Sector I

There is but One God
Who is realised through the grace of the True
* Guru.*

In the company of the Holy if you adore the
* Lord,*
The ills of a million births will depart.
You will obtain whatever you claim.
With God's grace you will be blessed with the
* Name.* (1)

The Name brings peace and fame as a prize,
With Guru's blessings has Nanak come to
* realise.* (2)

(720)

Raga Suhi

Suhi V

Dear my God! Your sight sustains.
Thus my cherished dreams I gain.
Dear my Lord! pray listen to me.
Bestow on me the Name and make
  me a devotee. (1)

My Benevolent Master! keep me by Your side.
With the Guru's grace that few realise. (2)

Dear my friend! do give me Your ear.
By Your lotus feet I may adhere. (3)

Nanak has only one prayer to offer,
I should forget not the virtuous self-contained
  coffer. (4)

(741–42)

Suhi V

Blessed is the hut where I sing His praises.
The mansion where He is forgotten may go to
  blazes.

Blessed is the poverty where in Holy company
    God is remembered.
Accursed is the ego with Maya encumbered. (1)

Covered with work-sheet, milling grindstone and
    feeling peaceful and contented,
What use is worldly power if it leaves one
    disgruntled. (2)

It is respectable going about naked in His bliss,
Of no use are silk and silken garments that
    lead you to avarice. (3)

Everything is in Your hands O Lord, You do
    and get things done.
That I should remember You every breath,
    Nanak asks this boon. (4)

                                          (745)

Suhi V

Those involved in the ritual of Karma and
    Dharma
Are booked by the tax collector, Yama.
One who is devoted to absolute adulation of
    the Creator,
A moment's remembrance of Whom serves as a
    liberator.
The Holy cruise through the ocean.
He who abides by the Holy,
He is ferried across with the Guru's
    benediction (1)

Bathing at millions of places of pilgrimage
Purifies not in the Kaliyug.
He who sings His praises in the company of
*   the Holy,*
He is sanctified (along with the family.) (2)

The reading of the Vedas, Islamic Scriptures,
Smrities and the Shastras does not obtain
*   Salvation.*
The devotee who contemplates on the Word,
He commands all-around ovation. (3)

The Kshatriyas, Brahmins, Shudras and the
*   Vaishyas,*
All the four castes have a common Gospel to
*   unfold.*
The devotee who remembers the Name in
*   Kaliyug is saved,*
Says Nanak, the Lord dwells in every soul. (4)

                                    (747–48)

Suhi V

He whom You protect, O Master!
How can he come to grief?
Maddened with Maya, he knows not how to
*   talk,*
Even death he does not conceive.
My Lord! You belong to the Holy and the Holy
*   to You.*
Your devotee fears not; him the Yama can't
*   pursue. (1)*

Those dedicated to You, they die not, nor are
  they born.
None may undo Your reprieve that the True
  Guru has sworn. (2)

They repeat the Name and are blessed with
  peace.
They remember You all the eight hours.
Under Your protection, depending upon You,
  they harness
The five malicious powers. (3)

Ignorant, not used to contemplation, without
  good deeds,
With You I remained unacquainted.
Supreme is Guru Nanak who blessed me,
And has had me fully sated. (4)

(750)

Suhi V

Octets to the tune of Kafi
Sector 10

There is but One God
Who is realised through the grace of the True
  Guru.

Maybe I am mistaken and misled
Yet I remain Yours.
Those who cultivate others,
Die suffering like the whores.
I will never forsake my Lord.
Ever lively, ever loving, He is my Eternal
  Ward. (1)

You are my friend, You are my kin,
You are indeed my pride.
With You I am ever happy;
Without You a snide. (2)

If You are gracious my Supreme Benefactor,
Let me not from Your path depart.
Let me cling to the gift of Your Name,
And treasure it in my heart. (3)

I should go Your way and bear You in mind.
With my ears I should hear Your discourse,
If my Guru were to be kind. (4)

Dear my Lord! millions and millions of (great)
*   men*
Compare not with a strand of Your hair.
To fathom the King of kings
How do I dare? (5)

You have no end of admirers,
They are far superior to me.
Do be kind for a trice,
Let me have a glimpse of Thee. (6)

How do I forget Him, my Mother
Whom all around I see. (7)

I fell at His feet in utter humility,
I met Him in the stride.
Maybe I owe it to my earlier deeds,
Nanak, the Holy, was my guide. (8)

(761)

Raga Suhi, Chhant V

There is but One God
Who is realised through the grace of the True
Guru.

Listen O insane! You are misled by what you
see.
Listen O insane! Your attachments are false
Like the colour of the flowers of a Kasumbda*
tree.
The delusion you see is of little value
It's God's Name alone which is of colour fast.
If you were to contemplate on the Sweet Word
of the Deity,
You will acquire the colour of dark red poppy.
Lost in false attachments, clinging to false
mores,
Nanak has come to the ocean of Grace;
Pray ferry me across to the shore. (1)

Listen O insane! Serve Him who is the Master
of life-breath.
Listen O insane! He who is born must end in
death.
Listen O wayfarer! Even the everlasting must
cease.
Cultivate the Holy and live in peace.
Listen O recluse! It is Karma that attracts the
Divine Beau.

---

*   Safflower

One must hold fast on to the feet of the Guru.
Listen O the Guru-conscious! Dedicate yourself
to the Supreme Guide.
Without any reservation, without any pride.
Nanak the humble, craves for the One who
ferries one across.
How can he praise well enough such a
Gracious Boss? (2)

Listen O insane! What for is this vain row?
Listen O insane! All the pride and conceit must
go.
Go we must, false is the ego, serve alone the
Godmen.
If it is destined, one lives in death and cruises
across the ocean.
Serving the Guru is like sipping Amrit
Which helps one acquire poise.
Nanak sought shelter at the Lord's Portal
Unto Whom he is ready for sacrifice. (3)

Listen O insane! Don't you believe you alone
have imbibed God.
Listen O insane! Be humble as dust
before those who contemplate on the Lord.
Those who contemplate on the Lord, they are
at peace.
Those who contemplate are at peace, the lucky
have a glimpse of the Divine.
One should be humble, ever sacrificing,
Forsaking all the ego of the mind.

For Him one would himself sell
The lucky one who has found God.
Nanak, the humble, pleads with the Ocean of
  Peace,
Vindicate my honour, O Lord! (4)

                                                                    (777)

Suhi V

God has bestowed on you the support of His
  lotus feet.
One should be sacrifice unto Him.
His coffers overflow with Amrit, where there is
  every treat.
One should be sacrifice unto Him.
My Father is mighty powerful,
He does and makes others do.
Remembering Him no sorrow afflicts,
He ferries one through the ocean.
He has protected devotees since eternity,
I live singing His praises in utter solemnity. (1)

Says Nanak, sweet is the elixir of His Name,
Day and night I drink in draughts.
God Himself effects the Union,
How can one be parted from Him?
One should be sacrifice unto Him.
He who has His support,
Forever he is fated to live.
One should be sacrifice unto Him.
Your support I gained and only from You,
The True Creator!
Without Whom there is none,
Varily such is my Maker.

Singing songs of joy day and night,
The Holy are hopeful.
To Him Nanak is sacrifice
Whose glimpse is ever fruitful. (2)

Cherishing the Holy abode, I gained honour,
* glory and truth.*
I am sacrifice unto Him.
I met the Gracious Master and sang praises of
* the Immortal forsooth.*
I am sacrifice unto Him.
I adored the Lord God day in and day out,
Who is the Beloved Lord of life.
Auspicious are the times,
He pulled me to His bosom.
And I met the reader of my inner strife.
Trumpets of truth and contentment resounded
* like the unstruck melody.*
Nanak listened and was relieved of fears by his
* All-Powerful Deity.* (3)

I was enlightened and realised truth of the One
* of every Age.*
I am sacrifice unto Him.
The created met the Creator, none could
* disengage.*
I am sacrifice unto Him.
It is wondrous what I behold, wondrous what I
* hear,*
And wondrous what I realise.

The Lord God prevails in the ocean and earth.
He lives in the one from where the one
  emerged.
His merit cannot be assessed,
Nanak meditates on the one
Whose doings are not manifest. (4)

(777–78)

Raga Suhi, Chhant V

There is but One God,
He is realised through the grace of the True
  Guru.

You are the Master, continent in spirit.
You have many a devotee the like of me.
You are the ocean full of pearls.
I know not Your extent.
Your extent I know not, You are Wisdom
  Incarnate.
Pray, do me a favour.
Bless me with such understanding
That I remember You day and night.
I should not be conceited; and remain humble
And thereby gain salvation.
Says Nanak, my Master is Supreme,
He has many a devotee the like of me it
  seems. (1)

You are fathomless, deep and profound.
You are the groom, I am Your bride.
You are big, the biggest of all.
I am small, small like a mite.
I am nobody; it is only You.

You are Omniscient.
A fleeting glance of the Divine You is life-giving.
I enjoy all the delights and pleasures.
I am the dust of Your feet and the slave of
    Your slaves.
My mind is invigorated and my body has
    blossomed.
Nanak's Master pervades all over.
He does whatever meets His favour. (2)

I am proud of You, You are my support.
My perceptions, wit and wisdom are Your gift.
I learn what You teach.
Only he knows and understands
Who is blessed by You, the Creator.
The self-willed is misled in a maze
And is caught in the network of Maya.
She who is acceptable to the Master is
    virtuous,
She alone enjoys the delights of life.
My Master! You are the support of Nanak,
You are Guru Nanak's pride. (3)

I adore You.
I am sacrifice unto You.
You screen me (from evil) like a mountain.
I am sacrifice unto You a million times,
Who has dissipated my clouds of doubt.
Darkness dispelled, free of misdeeds,
My mind is attuned to the Master.
Loved by the Lord, I become self-reliant.
A life successful, I become acceptable.

Invaluable, estimated high,
Flung open the doors of liberation and the
living-art.
Says Nanak, I became fearless.
The Preceptor took me into His heart. (4)

(780)

Suhi V

Do be gracious, my Beloved Master!
I long to have a glimpse of You.
Grant me a lakh of tongues, my Dear,
So that I repeat Your Name ever.
Repeating Your Name I should fear not Yama,
And suffer no affliction.
Master! You prevail in the ocean and earth.
Let me find You whichever direction I turn.
My doubts, attachments and misdeeds undone,
I should find my Lord closer than the closest.
Do be gracious to Nanak, O Lord!
I long to have a glimpse of God. (1)

Dear Lord! Grant me a million ears,
That I may listen to the praises of the
Immortal.
Listening to the praises my mind may be
cleansed,
And thus the noose of Yama snapped.
With the noose of Yama snapped and
remembering the Immortal,
I may be blessed and enlightened.
Let me remember God day and night
And dissolve into the poise of meditation.

Contemplating on God may free me of my
  sins and sufferings
And malice in my mind.
Says Nanak, Lord do be so gracious,
That I may always hear the praises sublime. (2)

May I have millions of hands to serve You,
And feet to tread Your path.
Serving God is like taking a boat in the ocean
  of life;
He who embarks it goes across.
Across the ocean, remembering the Lord
All the wishes are met,
Cardinal misdeeds undone, peace prevails,
And trumpets of delight are sounded.
I gained all the fruits I wanted.
Beyond limit is the Lord's prowess.
Says Nanak, do be gracious to me, Lord,
I may ever tread Your path. (3)

It is a blessing, it is a glory,
Only the lucky acquire this boon.
It is delightful, it is pleasure-giving,
Getting attached to His feet.
The Creator is the motivating force.
I am without merit, my Beloved is the Ocean
  of Peace.
My mind is awakened in the company of the
  Holy.
Says Nanak, the Lord is gracious,
I am attached to His lotus feet. (4)

(780–81)

Suhi V

Eternal is the town of the Divine Master
Where remembering the Name brings peace.
One finds there whatever one craves for.
The Creator Himself has founded it.
The Creator founded and blessed it with peace.
Sons, brothers and fellow devotees are
  delighted.
Singing praises of the Lord God
Every task has come to be accomplished.
He is the Master, He is the Saviour,
He is the Father and Mother.
Says Nanak, I am sacrifice unto the Deity
Who has founded this beautiful city. (1)

Houses, temples and bazaars look pleasant,
Reverberating with the Name as they do.
Saints and sages recite the Name
And thus snap the noose of death.
The noose of death is snapped by the Immortal
  Himself
For those who contemplate on the Name.
Everything obtains here;
One gets whatever one desires.
The friendly Godmen have a happy time.
All ills, afflictions and doubts disappear.
The Great Guru endows the Divine Word.
Nanak is sacrifice unto the Lord. (2)

The Master has kept His promise;
His favours multiply every day.
The Preceptor has taken me over,
He who is lauded everywhere.
The Lord who has protected the Holy from
    times primordial
Has been Merciful.
Every living creature has been accommodated.
God Himself has provided for them.
The Master is lauded all over.
It's difficult to measure His quality.
Nanak is sacrifice unto Him
Who has founded this Eternal city. (3)

Here one contemplates on the Lord,
Listens to His discourse day and night and is
    enlightened.
Mysterious are the doings of the shatterer of
    the worldly attachments.
Here one hears the unstruck melody.
Hearing the unstruck melody, contemplating on
    Truth
And a daily dialogue with the Holy,
Reciting the Name helps cleanse impurities
And shed all sins.
It frees from the cycle of life and death,
    coming and going;
No more transmigration of the soul.
Nanak is blessed by his Guru
Whose grace makes his wishes come true. (4)

(783)

Suhi V

He partook in the task of the Holy.
The Lord Himself came and gave a hand.
Blessed is the land, blessed is the Pool
Overflowing with Amrit.
Filled with water the like of Amrit
The project came to be completed
And the objective realised.
There is rejoicing all over,
Sorrows have fled.
The Lord God who is Perfection Incarnate,
*   Eternal and Immortal,*
Whose praises the Vedas and Puranas have
*   sung.*
Came to help Nanak who had His Name on
*   his tongue.* (1)

The Creator bestowed 'Nine   Treasures' and
*   'Mystic Powers' on me,*
Nothing was left to desire,
It was a pleasure, consuming, spending and
*   enjoying.*
Ever more are the Creator's gifts.
Ever more, there is no end to them.
This is how we realised the Omniscient.
Millions of mishaps, they were averted.
No ill afflicted.
It was peace, poise and utmost pleasure,
All my needs were met.
Nanak sang praises of the Lord
Whose greatness is beyond his words. (2)

Himself He accomplished whose task it was.
Man is a mere helpless creature!
Singing His praises the holy make a pleasant
*   spectacle;*
They glorify Him ever.
Sitting in Godmen's company
They derive pleasure in the Master's praises.
Those who have helped build, the Pool.
Their praise is beyond reckoning.
(The Pool embodies in itself the blessings of)
Sixty-eight places of pilgrimage, charities and
*   good record.*
My Master saves the sinners; it is His way.
Nanak is sustained by His Word. (3)

My Lord, my Creator is the Mine of Virtues.
He is far above adulation.
The Holy have only one prayer to make:
Master! Bestow on us the ecstasy of the
*   Name.*
Bestow on us the Name as Your charity
So that we forget You not for a moment.
We should sing Your praises with the tongue
And do it day and night.
He who is devoted to the Name,
His mind and body remain soaked in Amrit.
Nanak supplicated and had his desire met;
Now in the Lord's presence he is kept. (4)

(783–84)

Suhi V
Chhant

There is but One God
He is realised through the grace of the True
  Guru.

My Beloved Master is sweet-tongued.
He is not known to speak ill ever.
Speaks not ill, the Perfect Lord,
Nor does He notice evil.
To those gone astray, it is His way to retrieve.
Not for a moment He belittles the virtuous
  deed.
He lives in every heart; He who prevails all
  over.
He is nearer than the nearest.
Nanak remains in His presence ever;
He is as sweet as Amrit.
His beatific glimpse! And I am in rapture.
My Master is Charm Incarnate,
I am the dust of His feet.
I live by His sight; It relieves me.
There is no one as big as He is.
In the beginning, in the end, as well as at
  present He prevails.
He is there in water and earth.
Contemplating on His lotus-feet, one swims
  across the ocean
And arrives at the shore across.
Nanak comes for shelter to the Lord Perfect
Whose extent remains a secret. (2)

Not for a moment I lose sight of my Beloved
Who is the support of my life.
It has been ordained by the True Guru
One must contemplate on the Eternal Lord.
The Name is obtained if the Godman blesses.
It frees us of the affliction of life and death.
It lends peace and poise and infinite joy,
Untying the knot of ego.
He lives in all (of us) and is above all.
He is beyond love and hate.
Nanak, the humble, has come to the Lord,
The Beloved Master Who sustains all. (3)

As a result of my constant search
I have come across the Immutable Abode.
Rejecting the evanescent, I attached myself to
*   the lotus-feet.*
The Lord is Eternal, I am His slave-girl.
He dies not, nor does He come and go.
He embodies Dharma, worldly success and
*   love;*
Whatever one desires one obtains.
The Vedas and the Smrities sing the praises of
*   the Creator.*
The Yogis, ascetics and sages contemplate on
*   Him.*
Nanak encounters the Merciful Master of the
*   game*
Only the fortunate recite His Name. (4)

(784–85)

Raga Bilawal

Bilawal V

It is all peace
Brought about by the Great Guru,
Ushering in weal
With unstruck melody. (1)

Gone are the woes, violations and worries.
Remembering the Lord, sins are washed.
It is time to enjoy the company of the comely.
Guru Nanak's status is elevated overly. (2)

(806)

Bilawal V

The Guru Supreme shielded (us) at both the
ends.
The Lord God took care of (our) ups and
downs.
All (our) objectives came to be accomplished.

(1)

Contemplating on the Name brought peace and
  poise;
Like washing the dust of the feet of the holy.
Ceased the coming and going; it was all quiet.
The suffering of birth and death ended.
Vanished the doubts and fears of Yama.
That He prevails in every heart, (I came to
  realise).
Nanak sought shelter of the Reliever of pain,
Finding His presence inside and out, time and
  again. (2)

(825–26)

Bilawal V

. . .As the ray disappears in the Sun;
As the drop of water mixes with water;
A light dissolves in the Light
And comes to be consummated.
It is the Lord God we see.
It is the Lord God we hear.
It is He alone we have for discourse.
It is the Creator who is all over.
There is none other than the Lord God.
Himself He gives and receives Himself.
He is the cause of all happenings.
Says Nanak, only they realise it fine,
Who have tasted the Elixir Divine. (4)

(846)

Raga Gaund

Gaund V

Ever remember the Guru's Name.
There is none other than the Guru.
Seek the Guru's support day and night.
No one dare undo what He bestows.
The Guru and God are alike, it's true.
What He prescribes should be a boon for you.
  (1)

Those who are devoted to the Guru,
Their sorrows, afflictions and doubts vanish.
Serving the Guru brings glory.
One must be sacrifice unto the Guru. (2)

A glimpse of the Guru is exhilarating.
He who serves the Guru never fails.
The Guru's devotee comes not to sorrow.
The Guru's devotee is felicitated all over. (3)

It is not easy to fathom the Guru.
The Lord God himself reflects in the True.
He is fortunate, says Nanak, indeed.
He is dedicated to the Guru's feet. (4)

(864)

Raga Ramkali

Raga Ramkali V, Score I

There is but One God
Who is realised through the grace of the True
Guru.

Do be gracious, the Steward of the humble,
Pray, measure not my good or bad deeds.
What use is it to wash the clay!
Such is my plight.
O Man! Serve the True Guru and find peace.
One gains whatever one asks for.
No ill ever afflicts. (1)

He moulded and shaped unbaked pots
And lit them with candles.
Whatever was inscribed by the Creator,
I tried to do likewise. (2)

I reckoned the body and mind as mine,
And this led to my coming and going.
I remembered not the One who bestowed it all
And was engrossed in blind attachments. (3)

He who has created, He alone knows it.
Wondrous is the Mansion of the Lord.
I contemplate on Him, I sing His praises,
Nanak is a slave of his God. (4)

(882–83)

Ramkali V

Some call Him Rama,
Others know Him as Khuda.
Some serve Him as Goswami,
Others remember Him as Allah. (1)

The Merciful ordains all that happens.
He takes kindly in His grace. (2)

Some bathe at Hindu temples,
Others go on Haj.
Some recite from the Vedas,
Others from the Quran.
Some wear the blue robes,
Others are clad in white. (3)

Some are called Turks,
Others are known as Hindus.
Some seek the heaven of Islam,
Others the celestial abode of Indra. (4)

Says Nanak, he who obeys His command,
He alone understands the secret of the Lord. (5)

(885)

Ramkali V

O Man! Why do you waver and vacillate?
The Lord gives all that one asks for.
One must remember the True Guru
Who wipes all the woes.
Contemplate on the Name,
It rids of all the sins and misdeeds.
Only they are endowed with the Divine passion
Who are destined for it.
They are freed from the lure of Maya
And treasure the Name splendid.
They concentrate on the One all the while
And abide by His Divine command.
Nanak asks for just one favour,
Grant me a glance of endearment, Master! (2)

(959–60)

Pauri

You give support
Where none else can help.
You protect in the fire of the womb.
Hearing Your Name the couriers of Yama flee.
The Guru's Word ferries (us) through
The unfathomable, turbulent ocean.
Those who feel thirsty
They partake of Amrit.
Singing praises of the Lord
Is the only virtue in Kaliyug.
The Kind Master fosters every breath;
No one seeking succour
Ever experiences thirst. (4)

(961–62)

Slok V

Hearing Your tidings, I was excited.
Reciting Your Name, my face was flushed.
Treading Your Path, I was at peace.
By the glimpse of the Guru, I was blessed.
The Name in my heart is like possessing
    a jewel.
I bought it not; it is a gift of the Guru.
My search is over, I am secure with my prize.
Nanak has gained the gift of life.

Pauri

He who is fortunate takes to His service.
He whose lotus (heart) is blessed by the Guru,
He is awake day and night.
Attached to His holy feet,
My doubts and fears fled.
The Guru gave me such a Sermon
That I conquered myself for good.
He who remembers Lord God,
He gets known in the world.
He gains the company of the Holy,
And is cleansed as by bathing in sixty-eight
    places of pilgrimage.
He is fortunate who has access to his Lord.
Nanak is sacrifice unto his Gracious God. (17)

(964–65)

Raga Maru

Maru V

Ego, attachment, avarice and evil, I did not
*   indulge in.*
I traded in the Name alone as my goods that I
*   loaded and made a move.*
The devotee's devotion bore fruit in the end.
I served my Master as long as I lived,
And had Him in my mind when I departed. (1)

Whatever the Lord ordained, I evaded not.
I was at peace and in poise when asked to
*   stay on,*
And I rose to run when I was told to move. (2)

If He asked me to go hungry, I accepted it
*   with pleasure.*
I know not what is joy and sorrow.
Whatever was ordained by the Master,
I accepted it with a smile. (3)

The Lord took kindly to His devotee.
I was taken care of here and hereafter.
Blessed is the devotee, his visit is fruitful,
Says Nanak, who has imbibed the Master
　　Merciful. (4)

(1000)

Maru V, Sector 4 Ashtpadi

There is but One God
Who is realised through the grace of the True
　Guru.

Better than illuminating the courtyard, is the
　enlightenment of the heart. (1)

Of all the devotions, the best is the devotion to
　God. (2)

Amongst things to abjure,
It is better to give up lust, anger and
　avarice. (3)

If you must ask, beg the Guru for devotion to
　the Lord. (4)

Of all the vigils, the best is the one devoted to
　singing praises of the Master. (5)

The noblest devotion is devotion to the feet of
　the Lord. (6)

*He who is fortunate, only he comes to be
  favoured with these.* (7)

*Says Nanak, he is blessed with .the best,
Who comes under protection of his Deity.* (8)

Maru V

*Come, do please come,
I long to hear my Lord's praises.
When you are here I feel refreshed
Adoring the Lord in your company.* (1)

*With the grace of the Holy, I imbibe the Lord
And shake off my duality.* (2)

*I was enlightened when favoured by godmen
And shed the sickening evil thought.* (3)

*A glimpse of the Guru and I got cleansed,
I am free from having to be born again.* (4)

*He is blessed with the 'Nine Treasures' and
  'Mystic Power'
He whom You endear.* (5)

*I have no place other than the Guru's,
I know not where else to go.* (6)

*Without any merit, no one takes my care,
I long for the company of godmen.* (7)

*Says Nanak, the Guru showed me the way,
I enjoy remembering His Name and pray.* (8)

Maru V, Solahe (sixteen-stanzaed hymns)

There is but One God
Who is realised through the grace of the True
Guru.

Infatuated with him she is,
Deeply involved, enjoying love-plays.
Their past deeds have brought them together,
They indulge in carnal pleasures (1)

What he does, she must accept.
He keeps her in good humour.
They are together day and night,
There is nothing that she lacks. (2)

What she asks, he tries his best
And brings to her what he finds.
But one thing remains beyond his reach,
For which she ever pines. (3)

She prays with both her hands folded:
Pray! don't go away, stay at home,
That quenches my thirst and hunger. (4)

They do all the good deeds prescribed,
But without passion for the Lord
They find not a sesame of bliss.
But with His grace when they met Nanak,
Both he and she were exhilarated. (5)

It is all a game of five elements,
What one looks for obtains with the Guru. (6)

Says she: You must abide by me.
My comfort-loving, cherished beloved,
Without you the life has no meaning.
Pray, promise, you will not leave me. (7)

Says he: I live, but in His discipline;
He is the Great Master, Fearless and Supreme.
I will live with you as long as He permits,
When called, I must leave and quit. (8)

What he tells her is the truth;
But immature and restless she accepts it not.
She asks for his company again and again;
He laughs it away every time. (9)

Then he is summoned;
He neither asks her,
Nor does he take her into confidence;
He just leaves her widowed.
Says Nanak, it was all false attachment. (10)

My coveting mind, listen to me.
Serve the True Guru day and night.
Without the True Guru the godless are undone,
They have the noose of death round their neck.
(11)

The egoist comes, the egoist goes,
The egoist is buffeted again and again.
He has to undergo every hell,
The Guru-conscious has no sorrow to tell. (12)

He is Guru-conscious who is endeared by the
   Lord.
Who can undo him who is protected by His
   favour?
The blessed one remains ever in bliss,
He who is endowed with the robe of honour
   (13)

I am sacrifice unto the Great Guru
Who gives shelter and keeps His promise.
I have found my Lord, Bestower of Joy,
There is no more parting in His employ. (14)

He is the Mine of Virtue, He cannot be
   measured.
He dwells in every heart and every place.
Says Nanak, the humble, I have come to the
   protection of the Pain-Reliever,
I am the dust of the feet of such a
   Redeemer. (15)

(1072–73)

Maru V

O Yokel! Don't be misled by appearance.
It is all false love, it is an illusion.
No one lives in the world for ever.
The Lord alone is Eternal. (1)

Come to the protection of the Endowed Guru,
Give up attachments, anxieties and doubts.
Contemplate on the Name, that is the only
   Sermon, only remedy. (2)

The Name for which many a gods yearns.
He Whom all godmen serve.
Helper of the helpless
And Reliever of the sufferings of the humble
*   and true;*
He is imbibed only through the grace of the
*   Guru.* (3)

There is no other shelter,
None is found in the three spheres.
The True Guru is the bank with a
*   treasure of the Name,*
The jewel of Name can be had from Him
*   alone.* (4)

The dust of His feet cleanses:
Even the celestial beings cannot have it.
He is transparent, truthful, the Supreme Lord:
Propitiating Him and one swims across (the
*   ocean of life).* (5)

Man! if you are looking for Parjat,*
Remember Kamdhenu** adorns His Court.
You have to be content, patient and serve the
*   Endowed Guru;*
And take the exercise of contemplation
Which is like alchemy. (6)

---

   * Wish-fulfilling mythical tree
** Wish-fulfilling mythical cow

The Guru's Word destroys the source of five
   evils.
The fear of God purifies.
When the Great Guru favours with the touch
   of philosopher's stone,
He sees for himself the change. (7)

He cares not for Heaven, one or more.
The enlightened one cares not even for
   salvation, whatever it is worth.
The Holy Preceptor is imbibed through the
   True.
One is sacrifice unto a glimpse of such a
   Guru. (8)

No one knows how to serve the Master;
Only the Guru knows the One beyond senses.
   One can serve if He allows,
The one who is destined for it. (9)

Even the Vedas know not greatness of the
   Guru,
They describe a little they have heard about.
The Lord God is beyond reach, it is the True
   Guru
Contemplation on Whom calms the heart. (10)

He whose tidings are life-giving,
If He dwells in the heart, one is satisfied.
If the Guru-conscious contemplates on Him,
He is glorified and does not have to go the
   way of the Yama. (11)

I seek protection of the Holy.
Dedicating my life to them
I know not how to serve;
Lord! Be merciful to the worm I am. (12)

Take the meritless in Your company,
Be kind and let me serve You.
Waving the fan, grinding grain,
And washing Thine feet, (let me) find peace.
  (13)

I have knocked several doors.
I seek for Your favour and Your protection.
Pray, grant me the company of godmen,
And bless me with Thy Name as charity. (14)

The Master took kindly (to me).
I had a glimpse of the Endowed Guru.
Nanak, the slave of slaves, gained peace
And Eternal Joy from his Beau. (15)

(1077–78)

Maru V

Oh you! The follower of Allah, the Inaccessible
  Divine,
Forget about (your) worldly concerns.
You should be the dust of the feet of the
  Darvesh,
Only then you would be allowed at His
  door. (1)

Let truth be your Namaz[1] and faith be your
    Mussala.[2]
Kill (your) desires, that ought to be your Asa.[3]
Your body should be the Mosque
And your mind Maulana[4]
And your Divine Kalma[5] clean living. (2)

Your Shar'a[6] should be the way of God,
And your Tariqat[7] your quest for the Lord.
Marfat[8] should discipline your mind
And association with the Holy, your escape
    from death. (3)

Teaching of the Qura'n and scriptures should be
    part of your thinking,
And the ten mistresses held over from evil;
And the five men with faith.
Charity and contentment will make you
    acceptable to Him. (4)

Let Mehr[9] be your Mecca and humility your
    Raza*
And abiding by His Word opportunity for
    Bahisht.[10]
Let the Houries be enlightenment and Musk the
    devotion to God
And prayer be the exalted Hujra.[11] (5)

---

[1] Muslim prayer
[2] Prayer-mat
[3] Staff
[4] Priest
[5] Creed
[6] Code

[7] Pursuit of God
[8] Enlightenment
[9] Compassion
* Submission to God's will
[10] Heaven
[11] Closet

The Qazi[12] *is he who practises truth.*
The Haji[13] *is the one whose heart is disciplined.*
The Mulla[14] *is he who steers clear of evil*
  deeds.
The Darvesh is one, whose adoration of God is
  his creed. (6)

All the time, all the hours
The Maula[15] *must keep the Lord in his heart.*
Vanquishing the ten senses should be the
  Tasbih.[16]
Chaste and disciplined life his ritual Sunnat.[17] (7)

We must realise that everything is Filhalah.[18]
That the family (Khulkhana) is a snare.
That the rich and elite are mortal,
God is the only One who is Eternal. (8)

Adoration comes first, contentment next.
Humility is the third and charity fourth.
Fifth is the discipline of five senses.
These are your five sacred hours. (9)

---

[12] Judge
[13] Pilgrim
[14] Priest
[15] Master
[16] Rosary

[17] Discipline as practised
  by the Prophet
[18] Lasting for a short time
  (a passing phase)

Respect for every living being should be your
  Maudifa.[19]
The Kooja[20] *should be refraining from evil*
  deeds.
Your Baang[21] *should be call for the unity of*
  God,
And your trumpet subservience to Him. (10)

The food that you eat should be Haq-hallal.[22]
Your heart should be as big as a river
In which you should wash your filth.
He who venerates his Pir[23] *goes to heaven,*
Azrail[24] *does not condemn him to hell.* (11)

Your body should be a place of good character,
And the faith of a female,
So that you enjoy a truthful life.
The Hadis[25] *turning the impure into pure,*
And complete faith in Him is Dastar[26] *on your*
  head. (12)

He is a Muslim who is tender-hearted and pure.
He washes away impurities from his mind.
He does not involve himself in affairs of the
  world,
The way flower, silk and ghee[27] *do.*
He who is blessed by the Merciful

---

[19] Prayer
[20] Prayer jug
[21] Call for prayer
[22] Honestly acquired
[23] Elder

[24] An angel
[25] Tradition of
  Prophet Mohammad
[26] Turban
[27] Clarified butter

He is the man among men.
He is Sheikh,[28] *Musaik,*[29] *and Haji,*[30]
He to whom He takes kindly. (14)

Understanding the nature of the Creator and
the kindly Doer,
Adoring the Limitless, Benevolent Boss,
Accepting His command as truthful with faith,
Nanak earned his liberation and swam
across. (15)

(1083–84)

Maru Var V (Dakhne)

There is but One God
Who is realised through the grace of the True
Guru.

If You were to demand, my Love!
I'd sever my head and offer it to You.
My eyes yearn,
When do I have a glimpse of my Beau? (1)

It is to You I am committed,
All other attachments are false.
Dressing and eating for me become dreadful
If I don't have a glimpse of the True. (2)

---

[28] Hero
[29] Divine
[30] Pilgrim

To see You, my Love!
I get up early in the morn;
Kohl, necklace and the delight of eating betel
without seeing You have no charm. (3)

Pauri

You are the True Master.
You sustain the truthful ever.
You created and embellished the world,
For the righteous to live in it.
You had the Vedas produced
Which dwell on good and bad.
You created Brahma, Vishnu and Shiva
Who propagated the three Gunas.
Brought about the earth with nine continents
And shaped every part of it.
Produced varieties of creatures
And endowed them with life.
No one knows Your limit.
You are the True Creator.
You are in the know of all the ways
And You liberate those devoted to the
  Liberator. (1)

(1094)

Dakhne V

If You are a friend, distance me not for a
  moment.
My heart is enamoured of You, my Love!
When do I have a glimpse of You? (1)

*The evil-minded should burn and those causing
  separation should die.
Come my Love! Sleep on my bed,
And rid me of all my sorrow. (2)*

*('Evil-minded' is the duality and 'separatist' is
  the malady of ego.)
My Love is the True King,
Meeting Him is the life of joy.*

Pauri

*You are Inaccessible, Gracious and Limitless,
Who can measure Your merit?
You created the world.
You are the Master of the Universe.
No one understands Your ways.
My Lord who pervades all over,
No one dare approach You.
My Immortal, Who ferries us through the ocean
  (of the Universe),
You established the four Yugas.
You are the Maker of the world.
Coming and going is Your doing.
It makes not the slightest difference to You.
He to whom You are kind,
The True Guru takes him in His shelter.
There is no other way to imbibe You,
My Immortal, Creator of the world true.*

(1094-95)

Dakhne V

If You were to be in my courtyard,
The whole world will look pretty.
In the absence of my Master,
No one cares to look at me. (1)

Everything appears fine
When my Lord graces my premises.
Whoever visits this house
Does not go empty-handed. (2)

I laid out the bed for my spouse
And dressed in rich garments.
I would not wear a garland
(As it may distance me from my Friend.) (3)

Pauri

You are the Lord God, You are Immortal.
The Universe is created by Your command;
And maintained after creation.
No one can visualise Your image;
How does one contemplate on You?
You prevail everywhere,
And reflect in Nature Divine.
Your devotees have their treasures full,
There is no lack of anything;
Gems, jewels and diamonds
Which are beyond any price.
He takes to the service of the True Guru
To whom You take kindly.
He who adores the Lord and His praises chants,
He forsooth suffers no want. (3)

(1095)

Dakhne V

Look ahead.
Bother not about the past.
Says Nanak, live your life in a manner
That you do not have to be born again. (1)

My Love is such a fine sport,
He is a friend of all.
Everyone treats Him as his own,
He does not hurt any heart. (2)

I have discovered the Lord who had hid
  Himself,
I was destined I must say.
Says Nanak, blessed is the station
Where my Love has come to stay. (3)

Pauri

When You are on my side,
I lack nothing.
You endowed me with everything,
I am Your slave.
There is no end to wealth;
I keep consuming and spending.
The lakhs of people in the Universe
Serve You, all of them.
The foes have turned friends;
No one speaks ill.
When God has absolved,
Nobody dare ask the account.

I met the Supreme Guru,
I am happy, I have gained peace.
If He is pleased,
Everything turns out to be in form with ease.
  (7)

(1096)

Dakhne V

Those who I looked up to,
They seemed to seek me.
Those who I thought of asking for assistance,
They sought my help. (1)

Here is an unbaked bit of molasses,
They come flying in droves;
Those who sit on it are caught;
The one who can get away is lucky.
I have looked around everywhere,
There is no one without You.
He who contemplates on God,
I consider him lucky, my Lord.

Pauri

I would sing praises at His portal
If He so pleases.
My Lord is Eternal;
The rest come and go.
I ask the Master for a boon
Which quenches my hunger.
Dear Lord! Grant me a glimpse
Which should satisfy Your bard.

The Gracious Lord heard the prayer
And summoned the bard to His Mansion.
A glimpse, and the bard's hunger was satisfied.
The bard knew not what to ask for.
All his desires were fulfilled.
Falling at the Lord's feet,
The Lord God was softened.
The bard without merit and virtue was
*   pardoned.*

(1097)

Slok V

Accept first the death,
Forget the longing for life.
Before you come to us
You should be (as humble as) dust of
*   everybody's feet.* (1)

Consider Yourself dead in life.
Those living must die.
He who loves the Lord God,
He is exalted. (2)

He who meditates on the Preceptor,
He comes not to harm.
He is not tortured by hunger or thirst,
Neither is he tormented by Yama*
*   nor hurt.* (3)

---

*   The god of death

Pauri

He is beyond measure,
My Immortal, True Master.
The miracle-maker, the ascetic, the enlightened
  and those absorbed in meditation
No one can measure His worth.
He makes and breaks;
Produces and destroys;
He does and makes others do.
He breathes in every soul.
He provides for every creature.
Why must you vacillate?
He is deep, profound and unfathomable,
Full of rare virtues and enlightenment.
I do what the Master ordains from above
  forsooth.
Beyond Him there is nothing, Nanak tells the
  truth.

(1102)

Raga Tukhari

Chhant V

There is but One God
Who is realised through the grace of the True
  Guru.

I am sacrifice unto You, my Lord!
For blessing me with the Guru.
Listening to Your Holy Word
My heart has moved, True.
It is an attachment as of the fish with water.
Dyed in the dusky colour of the Master,
I fail to appraise You, my Lord.
Your status remains splendid.
My dear Purveyor of every virtue,
Listen to the plea of the one abandoned:
Pray, let me have a glimpse of my Beau.
Nanak is sacrifice unto You. (1)

This body is Yours, also the mind.
If I am good it is because You are kind.
I would fain give my life
To see You for the twinkling of an eye.

Listen, O Lord! seeing You for a trice
Gives a purpose to my life.
Your Name is said to be Amrit.
I drink it if only You permit.
I live, longing for my Preceptor
Like a Chatrik thirsting for a drop of water.
Says Nanak, I am sacrifice unto You,
Let me have a glimpse (of You), my Beau! (2)

You are the True Master, beyond any limit,
The Dear Beloved, to my life You are knit.
Known to the Guru-conscious, You are the
  Purveyor of peace.
Reflected in many colours,
Man does only what You please.
To whom the Creator is kind,
He endears himself to godmen.
Says Nanak, they are indeed a source of joy;
I remain ever sacrifice unto them. (3)

The Invisible cherished the ardent devotees,
The True Guru covered the sinner's frailties.
He who gave shelter is the Creator,
Sustainer of life breath and a peaceful living.
He is Immortal and Eternal Master;
A Perfect Entity, Maker and ever Giving.
No one can praise Him enough,
Nor know from where He came.
Nanak, the humble, is sacrifice unto Him
Praying for a fraction of His Name. (4)

(1117)

Raga Kedara

Kedara V

I long to see my Lord!
Pray, grant me Your Holy company,
Where I hear the Name of God.
Let me serve my Truthful Beau.
Listening to Him rejoices my heart.
I am ever sacrifice to You,
Who resides in a fair resort. (1)

You nourish and cherish one and all,
You give us all shelter.
You are Nanak's Lord Creator.
In every face he finds his Master. (2)

(1120)

Kedara V

I cherish my Beloved God;
Contemplating and full of dreams
My eyes long to see the Lord.
Blessed are the days, hours and minutes,
Blessed indeed are the seconds.
Enlightened in a moment with hopes bright,
I now live to see my Lord. (1)

(To attain Him) what effort and what measure,
What service do I contemplate?
Says Nanak, give up ego, conceit and
    attachments,
It is the Holy company that liberates. (2)

(1120)

Raga Bhairav

Bhairav V

Standing I am happy.
I am happy sitting.
He who has realised God
Afraid he is not. (1)

My only anchor is my Consort
Primed of every heart.
I sleep without anxiety,
Without anxiety I wake. (2)

Finding God here and there,
Everywhere without mistake.
Peace at home,
Peace outside.
Says Nanak, it is in my Guru's wake. (3)

(1136)

Bhairav V

Superb indeed is Your Name.
False is all the worldly fame.

Your creation is charming,
Your sight is warming.
Without Your Name
The world is a bane. (1)

Your nature is bewildering,
Your movements a marvel.
The righteous serve You,
Your virtue is unequalled. (2)

You are Shelter of the shelterless.
A Protecting Lord.
Sustainer of the poor,
Day and night I remember You, O God! (3)

Says Nanak, the Master Himself took kindly to
    him.
He forgot him not even in His whim. (4)

                                                    (1138)

Bhairav V

Ego is a human vice,
Lust of the elephant.
The moth go to the light and dies,
And sound nets the deer tight. (1)

The fish is caught for taste of the tongue,
The bumble bee for the sense of smell.
Attachment is the bane of us all,
The Three Evils make living a hell. (2)

You die in suffering.
In suffering are you born.
Condemned to suffering, the soul transforms.
Afflicted with maladies the man has no peace.
Without the True Guru the malady won't
  cease. (3)

He to whom the Creator takes kindly,
He pulls him out of the malady.
Snapped are Nanak's bonds,
Company of the Holy (he has) gained,
And freedom from suffering he has obtained. (4)

(1141)

Bhairav V

He should die in shame,
He who does not recite His Name.
Without the Name how can one rest in peace?
Without the Name there is no release.
Shoots will not sprout if the soil does not
  please.
I must remember my Supreme Lord
Who washes the filth of ages;
Snaps the bonds, ties (me) to God. (1)

Washed at a place of pilgrimage
How could a brimstone be clean?
Like the mind smeared with ego
(Remaining ever conceited and mean.)
Whatever he does, he remains bound;
Without the Name, it is all waste, unsound. (2)

Without eating, one's hunger is not quenched.
Until freed of malady one continues to be
wrenched.
Given to lust, temper, avarice and attachment
You cared not for the Creator and the
sacrament. (3)

Blessed are godmen, blessed is the Name;
Blessed are the day and night in acclaim.
Blessed is His devotion, blessed the Creator,
Nanak has adopted a wondrous Master. (4)

(1149)

Raga Basant

Basant V, Sector I

There is but One God
Who is realised through the grace of the True
  Guru.

Let us salute the Guru and serve Him.
It is an occasion of rejoicing.
There is supreme bliss around.
Anxieties allayed at Guru's offering.
It is spring time at our house, today;
To the Limitless Lord we get to Pray. (1)

We play Holi with the Lord.
Our Holi is to serve the Holy,
Dyed in the deep hues of Divinity. (2)

The mind and body are blooming like a
  meadow,
Unaffected by sunshine and shade.
Remaining green all the time
It is ever spring in the company of the
  Sublime. (3)

The (miracle) tree Parjat has sprouted,
Its flowers are like jewels.
Singing the Lord's praises we are satisfied,
Nanak, the slave, lauds the Lord as a rule. (4)

Basant V

There is but One God
Who is realised through the grace of the True
*   Guru.*

Behold! the flowers are in full bloom.
Forsaking conceit
Stick to the Lord's feet;
Get to the blessed bosom
Contemplating on the Creator.
The tender shoots are fragrant,
While others are dry and hard.
At the time of Basant
Everything is exuberant. (1)

It is Kaliyug now
The seed of Name you must sow.
No other time is opportune
Lest you make a mistake.
It is the Guru who gets to God,
He who has it written in his fate.
It is time to remember the Lord,
Nanak is smitten with the Name of God. (2)

(1185)

Basant V, Sector I

There is but One God
Who is realised through the grace of the True
*   Guru.*

Listening to the tales of the Holy
Remember the Lord with devotion.
Ajamal* was liberated by just one utterance.
Balmik** was blessed in the company of the
*   saintly.*
Dhruv, no doubt, imbibed Divinity.
I seek dust of the feet of Your devotee
To plaster my forehead, pray, do be kind to
*   me.* (1)

Ganka$^\#$ gained Salvation because her parrot
*   remembered God.*
Gajinder, the elephant, was granted deliverance
*   for praying to the Lord.*
Sudaman, the Brahmin, remained no more poor.
Man, you must meditate on such a Doer. (2)

---

* A Brahmin who lived with a prostitute. His
   son's name was Narain. By calling Narain, one
   of the names of God, he was saved.
** A robber who turned holy.
$^\#$ A prostitute.

Saved was the hunter who shot the arrow.
Kubja* was blessed by the (Lord's) foot on her
*   toe.*
Vidur** was free of his complex of servility.
O Man! You must also adore the Deity. (3)

God Himself vindicated Prahlad,
And robe he sent to Draupadi when His help
*   she sought.*
All of them remembered the Lord in peril.
Man! You must also serve Him
Who dwells across the channel. (4)

Dhanna served Him like a child.
Trilochan was enlightened by his Guru.
So did Beni.
O Man! You must also serve Him, true. (5)

Jaidev got rid of his ego.
Sain, the barber, served and was spared.
O Man! Don't you waver and go astray.
You, too, can be saved if you follow His way. (6)

Saved are the devotees to whom the Master
*   takes kindly.*
Their deeds good and bad are reckoned not.
Seeing this I come to Your care
And have Your shelter sought. (7)

---

* A deformed woman cured by Krishna
** A low-caste devotee of Krishna

Kabir meditated on Him devotedly.
Namdev remained in the presence of God.
Ravidas remembered the Master Incomparable.
Guru Nanak is truly the image of God. (8)

(1192)

Raga Sarang

Sarang V

The Lord Himself fulfilled my desires,
Invoking Him I got everything.
I remembered Him round the clock.
Master! Your Name is like Amrit.
He who sips it (his thirst) is quenched.
His sins of ages are washed.
And in the end he is liberated. (1)

You are Supreme, Perfection Incarnate and
*   Immortal Lord!*
I come to seek Your shelter, my Creator.
Pray let me propitiate at Your feet.
Nanak's mind and body long for a glimpse of
*   the Master. (2)*

(1208)

Sarang V

My Charming Beau! Pray do come home, I
*   crave.*
I am proud and talk loud;
Mistaken and misled and yet I am Your slave.

I hear You are close;
Suffering from duality I see You not.
Do be kind and remove the curtain,
Yearning for You is my longing heart. (1)

If I were to forget You for an instant,
It appears millions of days and years have
passed.
When he found the company of the Holy
Nanak met in them his God. (2)

(1209)

Sarang V

My tongue utters just Your Name.
You who fostered me in my mother's womb,
In the land of death would do the same.
You are the father, You are also the mother.
You are the loving friend and brother.
You are the family, You are the base,
You have given me life and breath in grace. (1)

You are the treasure rich with funds,
You are all the gems, jewels and diamonds.
You are the Parjat obtained from the Guru.
Nanak, the blessed, is grateful to You. (2)

(1215)

Sarang V

O Master! I come in Your care;
The moment I had Your glimpse
All my fears became scarce.

You knew my plight without (my) uttering a
  word
And made me recite Your Name.
Ended my woes, You gave me peace and poise,
I sang Your praises in a joyous frame. (1)

How was Nanak's bondage terminated?
In from the dark dungeon of Maya
You held his hand, pulled him out.
And helped him meet the Long-Separated. (2)

                                    (1218-19)

Sarang V

The Scriptures occupy the status of God.
Singing praises of the Creator in the company
  of the Holy
The mind is fully enlightened by the Lord.
The ascetics, miracle-makers and the sages
  yearn,
But few do His secret learn.
He whom He takes kindly,
He alone succeeds finally. (1)

He whom the Formless favours,
He comes to be known the world over.
Not for a moment should I forget the Divine,
A boon for which Nanak pines. (2)

                                    (1226)

Raga Malhar

Malhar V

Pour like a cloud,
Pray, delay it not for a moment,
Dear my Beloved Lord.
Longing for ever, let me be heartened.
You are my only support.
Forget me not, my Master!
The wife is bonded for life;
Without the spouse she is an utter disaster. (1)

When my Lord listened to the Prayer,
Post-haste He came in grace.
Says Nanak, I am happily married now,
All my problems are in place. (2)

(1268)

Malhar V

Lord God, Gracious, Merciful!
Sustainer, Cherisher of the helpless,
Pray, banish the suffering of the humble. (1)

All Powerful, Perfection Incarnate, Inaccessible!
Do be graceful. (2)

Plunged in the terrible dark well,
Says Nanak, pray, out me pull. (3)

(1273)

Raga Kanada

Kanada V

I have shed all my malice
Ever since I have cultivated the Holy.
I have no enemy nor any alien,
With everyone I find myself friendly. (1)

Whatever the Lord does, I welcome;
I have gained this wisdom from the
*   Almighty.* (2)

The Lord God prevails all over.
Nanak watches Him and feels happy. (3)

(1299)

Kanada V

Lord! You alone are my anchor.
You are my pride, You are my ego.
You are my support, I seek Your shelter.
You are my hope, I rely on You.
I have Your Name in my heart's quarter.
You are my might, I enjoy Your company.
Whatever You ask, I do, O! my Mentor. (1)

Your compassion and kindness bestow
  peace on me.
If You are gracious, the ocean I conquer.
You blessed me with fearlessness,
Nanak offers his head to such a Master. (2)

(1299–1300)

Slokas

Slok V

If wings were on sale, I'd barter;
Pinning them on to my limbs, I'd look for my
  Master (21)

My Lord is the True King,
He is the King of kings.
Sitting by His side is a matter of pride,
He gives everyone wings. (22)

Mundawani

Truth, contentment and contemplation;
There are three delicacies in this plate.
Also the Amrit of the Lord's Name,
Which caters to every taste.
He who partakes of this fare,
He would ever be surfeit.
This is something you can't do without,
Cherish it as a fact.
The grace of His feet
Ferries you through the dark world,
Says Nanak, it is all the Lord's estate.

(1429)

Slok V

I know not Your ways,
Worthy of it all You have made me.
Worthless I was, without any merit.
With Your grace You have swayed me.
Mercifully You are benevolent
And I met the True Guru.
Nanak now lives on the Name alone,
His mind and body are blessed, true. (1)

(1429)

Glossary

Ajamal. A Brahmin who lived with a prostitute. His son's name was Narain. By calling 'Narain', one of God's name, he was saved.

Ajpa Jaap. Reflex action in remembering the Lord

Akshra. Word.

Allah. God.

Asa. Staff.

Asadh. The fourth month of the Indian Calendar.

Assu. The seventh month of the Indian Calendar.

Azrael. An angel.

Baang. Call for prayer.

Bahisht. Heaven.

Baisakh. The second month of the Indian Calendar.

Balmik. A robber who turned holy and wrote the Ramayana

Baoli. Open well with steps to reach the surface of water.

Bani. Sikh scriptures.

Bhadon. The sixth month of the Indian Calendar.

Bhagwan. The Lord God.

Bhakti. Devotion.

Bhoingam. Yogic exercise.

Bohitha. Ship, ferry.

Chatrik. The rain bird.

Chet. The first month of the Indian Calendar.

Chitragupta. The god who is said to maintain an account of one's deeds.

Darbar. Court.

Dastar. Turban.

Deva. God, Guru.

Dharamraja. The god of judgement.

Dharamsala. Shrine; place of worship.

Dhayana. Meditation.

Dohta. Grandson; daughter's child.

Filhalah. Lasting for a short time.

Four Yugas. Four ages of the cosmos.

Ghee. Clarified butter.

Gobind. God.

Ganka. A prostitute.

Hadis. Tradition of the Prophet Mohammad.

Haji. Pilgrim.

Haq-hallal. Honestly acquired.

Hari. God.

Hujra. Closet.

Jakha. Mythical spirit.

Jeth. The third month of the Indian Calendar.

Kaliyug. The last of the four ages of the cosmos.

Kalma. Creed.

Kamdhenu. A mythical wish-fulfilling cow.

Karma. That one is because of his own doings.

Kartik. The eighth month of the Indian Calendar.

Kasumbda. Safflower.

Kinara. Mythical spirit.

Kirt Karni. Honest labour.

Kooja. Prayer mug.

Kos. 2.4 kilometres, approximately.

Kubja. A so-called low caste devotee of Krishna.

Lashkar. Army.

Magh. The eleventh month of the Indian Calendar.

Maghar. The ninth month of the Indian Calendar.

Marfat. Enlightenment.

Maudifa. Prayer.

Maula. Master.

Maulana. Priest.

Maya. Materialism, ungodly urges.

Mehr. Compassion.

Miri. Polity.

Mulla. Priest.

Musaik. Divine.

Mussala. Prayer mat.

Nam. Name; divination.

Namaz. Muslim prayer.

Nine Treasures. Nine treasures of Kubera, the god of wealth.

Nirgun. Unattributed.

Nival. Yogic exercise to cleanse the bowels.

Niyoli Karma. A yogic exercise for cleaning bowels for better concentration.

Parbraham. Supreme Being, God.

Parjat. A mythical wish-fulfilling tree.

Parmeshwar. Creator.

Phagun. The twelfth month of the Indian Calendar.

Pir. Elder.

Piri. Piety.

Pisacha. Mythical low spirit.

Pokh. The tenth month of the Indian Calendar.

Pothi. The name given to the Sikh Scriptures (Guru Granth Sahib) at the time of compilation.

Qazi. Muslim Judge.

Qudrat Wassiya. Reflected in nature.

Raga. Musical measure.

Sagun. Attributed.

Sawan. Rainy season; The fifth month of the Indian Calendar.

Shar'a. Code.

Shabd. Word; Divine utterance.

Sahaj. A state of poise.

Shakti. Parvati; mother Goddess, feminine power.

Sheikh. Hero.

Sherbet. Sweet, cooling drink.

Shiva. The God who destroys.

Simran. Remembering God; living in the Divine presence.

Sridhar. Vishnu, Hari.

Sunnat. Discipline as practised by the Prophet.

Tariqat. Search after God.

Tasbih. Rosary.

Three Gunas. These are: Tamas (sloth, the darker urges), Rajas (Passion) and Satva (Poise).

Tilak. Consecration mark.

Turiya. The mental state of super-consciousness, samadhi.

Vaishanav. Followers of Lord Vishnu.

Wand Chhakna. Sharing with others.

Yama. Messenger of death.

Yogi. Recluse.